Finding
Diversity

Finding Diversity

A Directory of Recruiting Resources

Luby Ismail and Alex Kronemer

Society for Human Resource Management
Alexandria, Virginia
USA
www.shrm.org

The Society for Human Resource Management (SHRM) is the leading voice of the human resource profession, representing more than 165,000 professional and student members throughout the world. Visit SHRM Online at www.shrm.org.

ISBN: 1-58644-021-7

Printed in the United States of America.
10 9 8 7 6 5 4 3 2 1

CONTENTS

7061

CONTENTS

PREFACE

I t is often said that necessity is the mother of invention. That is certainly true of this book. Ten years ago, when we first provided diversity training to human resource personnel across the country, we often heard a common complaint. It wasn't about the importance of diversifying America's workforce; everyone we spoke to seemed to be convinced of that. And not about any of our recommendations on managing a multi-racial, multi-cultural, equally gendered workforce. It was actually something more basic: "We want to have a more diverse workforce," we would hear, "but we don't know where to advertise to reach qualified candidates."

We would sometimes suggest a few of the resources we knew of, but in all truth it was rather hit-and-miss. Then, at a particular training program, when one persistent attendee pushed us on the subject, we suggested that she consult a directory of diversity recruitment. Seeing that this answer satisfied her, we decided to bring a few such directories to our next training—to point to the next time the question was asked. So we searched for such a tool: a publication where employers could find out where to advertise employment opportunities in hopes of attracting a diverse array of people.

To our surprise, we could find no such a resource.

It was then that we decided to put together our own listing. At first it was just a couple dozen names included in a resource packet that we handed out. But this only stimulated requests for a more comprehensive listing.

In 1993, a year and many, many hours of research later, we self-published the first such listing, *The Directory of Diversity Recruitment*. Our first printing of 500 copies sold out in a couple of months. Since then, we have kept our printer busy and have updated the directory several times through the 1990s.

A few years ago, we began to realize that the need for this resource had grown beyond our own customers—it was becoming a major need for HR professionals. The shifting demographics in the United States and globalization have turned recruiting and retaining a diverse pool of talented people into a business necessity. Thus was born this new resource, *Finding Diversity: A Directory of Recruiting Resources*, which we hope will be an even better source of information to help employers achieve their goals and fulfill their commitments to diversity.

PREFACE

Finding Diversity provides you with more than 300 recruitment tools to consider for reaching a diverse audience with a wide range of skills, specialties, educational levels, and abilities. Our partnership with SHRM is with the intention to make the book accessible and available to the Society's 165,000 HR members. Valuing diversity begins with recruitment and with your ability as HR professionals to find qualified candidates to build a diverse, highly capable workforce for your organization—a key to maintaining a competitive advantage in both domestic and global markets.

We want to extend our appreciation to Jessica Gilbert, a diversity consultant and trainer, for her many good suggestions, hard work, and extensive knowledge about diversity recruitment that helped us identify some of the best resources available to bring to you.

We hope this book proves useful and that it helps bring you success in your recruitment initiatives. We welcome your feedback and suggestions; please send any comments to:

Luby Ismail or Alex Kronemer
Connecting Cultures
lismail@connecting-cultures.net
(301) 438-3153
www.connecting-cultures.net

HOW TO USE THIS BOOK

Welcome to *Finding Diversity: A Directory of Recruiting Resources*

Workplace diversity is no longer simply a moral or legal responsibility; it is the key to maintaining the competitive advantage in the domestic and global markets. The listings in *Finding Diversity* are some of the best places to recruit the high-quality staff that you need to succeed. When you use the publications, web sites, conferences, career fairs, and other resources listed here, you are expressing your commitment to equal opportunity and taking a step toward diversifying your workforce.

Sections of the Book

The information in the directory is arranged in several sections.

Section One

The first section presents listings in grid format, according to the following broad job categories:

- Advanced Technologies
- General Recruitment
- Managers and Executives
- Professionals

Within each category, tools are listed by their type:

- Electronic (for example, web sites, e-mail lists, electronic publications)
- On-site (for example, job fairs, conferences, resource centers)
- Print (for example, magazines, newsletters)

Brief descriptions of each tool help you make comparisons among them and help you determine which appear most suitable for your needs.

Section Two

The second section lists the tools alphabetically, by name, and gives full information about each tool, including audience characteristics, rate information, and contact numbers.

Section Three

To make the directory more useful, it also includes the following lists:

- By geographical coverage: for users interested in reaching a particular area.
- By type: showing all of the electronic, on-site, and print tools available, regardless of job category.
- By language: for employers seeking candidates with skills in languages other than English. This characteristic indicates that the audience for the tool may speak the language; it is not an assurance.
- By organization name: so that employers can easily find all of the tools offered by each organization.

About the Tools Chosen

The directory lists only recruiting tools that regularly accept job ads or include job openings as part of their material. Therefore, the book does not list resources that target diverse audiences but that are not likely to be consulted by job seekers for work opportunities. College and university job fairs and similar school resources also do not appear in the directory; in general, the listings reach people with at least some job experience. One criterion for inclusion was that a recruiting tool targets audiences that would be qualified to fill positions that might be advertised.

About the Information

All of the information in the book was supplied by the recruiting tools. Every effort has been made to ensure accuracy of all information and claims at the time of publication. However, the claims, especially those regarding the audience reached, *are not the directory's assessment of the audience.* This information should be used only as a reference. Rates and audience sizes change, and only a media kit or direct contact with the recruiting tool can determine if it reaches the audience that has the desired skills and experience you are seeking.

The addresses for web sites should be used exactly as given. For example, do not enter a "www" if the address is not given that way.

As noted under "Sections of the Book," *Finding Diversity* presents four broad work categories:

- Advanced Technologies comprises tools that target people with computer, engineering, mathematical, scientific, or other technical skills.
- General Recruitment describes tools that target a high-quality audience in a wide variety of skill areas.
- Managers and Executives includes tools targeted to readers who possess management and executive skills or individuals with higher income levels and significant academic and professional achievements.
- Professionals lists tools that reach people from various professional backgrounds or that are directed to an audience that includes a large number of professionals.

Placement of a listing in a particular category is more art than science. Determination was made on the basis of the largest audience the recruiting tool targets (or was likely to attract). To have the most comprehensive information on where to advertise, you should look at the listings in related categories. For example, some of the listings under "Professionals" may by useful when looking for a person to fill a manager or executive position. The same is true for "General Recruitment," which should be looked at as a source of possibilities for any position.

Arrangement of Information

Each full listing includes the following information:

Recruiting Tool. The listing starts with the name of the tool, the organization that produces it, and its general contact information. All contacts regarding advertising should go to the "Advertising Contact" listed later. The general contact information is for reference only.

Recruiting Section. This is the work category to which the tool has been assigned.

Type/Frequency. Gives the form of the tool and its frequency. "Frequency" for an electronic tool is how often it is updated. For an on-site tool it means how often the event occurs. For print tools "frequency" is how often the tool is issued.

Description. This section contains the self-description provided by the recruiting tool.

Circulation/Audited by. "Circulation" is the number of people that the tool claims to have in its audience. For electronic tools, this could be the number of visitors to a web site. For on-site tools, attendees at a conference. For printed tools, actual circulation. *It should be understood that this number is based on information provided by the tool itself.* If an independent, outside auditing agency verifies circulation, the name of that agency appears here.

Coverage. The primary geographic area reached by the recruitment tool. Web sites are, for the most part, described as "Global" because of their amorphous reach. That does not mean that the site actually attracts visitors from all over the world. "International" is used to describe printed tools that reach further than the United States.

Rates. The quoted rates are meant for use as a range estimate only, mainly to give you the ability to make an initial comparison on costs. Every tool has many different options and rates are subject to change. Contact the tool directly for most current rates and available discounts. The listed rates are the most current information available at the time of publication.

Audience Characteristics. When possible, information is given on characteristics of the recruitment tool's audience. The type of information given includes educational level, business, profession, and language spoken. A language listing means that the audience *may* speak the language indicated; it is not an assurance. See "About the Information" for further information about characteristics.

Advertising Contact. The person or department to contact for further information or to place an ad.

SECTION ONE

Recruiting Tools
by Category

Electronic

Recruiting Tool/ Type	Circulation/ Frequency	Coverage	Audience Characteristics
AISES.com American Indian Science and Engineering Society *Web site*	*Daily*	Global	• College Graduates • High-Tech • Engineering, Sciences
AWG E-Mail News Association for Women Geoscientists *E-mail newsletter*	*Daily*	Global	• Postgraduate Degree Holders • Higher Education • Sciences
AWG Web site Association for Women Geoscientists *Web site*	*Daily*	Global	• Postgraduate Degree Holders • Higher Education • Sciences
AWIS.org Association for Women in Science *Web site*	*Weekly*	Global	• Postgraduate Degree Holders • Sciences
BDPA Job Listings National Black Data Processing Associates *Web site*	*Daily*	Global	• College Graduates • High-Tech • Computers/Information Technology
BDPA Journal Online National Black Data Processing Associates *Web site*	*Quarterly*	Global	• College Graduates • High-Tech • Computers/Information Technology
CASPA Chinese American Semiconductor Professional Association *Web site*	1,000 *Monthly*	Global	• College Graduates • High-Tech • Computers/Information Technology, Sciences, Engineering • Chinese Language
Center on Employment National Technology Institute for the Deaf *Web site*	*Daily*	Global	• College Students/Recent Graduates
Committee on Women in Engineering IEEE - Institute of Electrical and Electronics Engineers *E-mail list*	*Monthly*	Global	• College Graduates • High-Tech • Computers/Information Technology, Technology

Electronic

Recruiting Tool/ *Type*	Circulation/ *Frequency*	Coverage	Audience Characteristics
CSPA.com Chinese Software Professionals Association *Web site*	2,000 *Daily*	CA	• College Graduates • High-Tech • Computers/Information Technology, Technology • Chinese Language
HeadsUp Black Geeks Online *E-mail list*	28,000 *Three times per week*	Global	• Advanced Technologies, Computers/Information Technology
IWITTS.com Institute for Women in Trades, Technology & Science *Web site*	*Daily*	Global	• Computers/ Information technology, Sciences, Advanced Technologies
NABTP.org National Association of Black Telecommunications Professionals *Web site*	*Daily*	Global	• College Graduates • High-Tech • Communications
NAMEPA.org National Association of Minority Engineering Program Administrators *Web site*	*Biannually*	Global	• College Graduates • High-Tech • Engineering
NAMIC National Association of Minorities in Communication *Web site*	*Daily*	Global	• College Graduates • High-Tech • Communications
NATEA North American Taiwanese Engineer Association *Web site*	600 *Monthly*	Global	• College Graduates • High-Tech • Computers/Information Technology, Engineering • Chinese Language
NOBCChE.org National Organization for the Professional Advancement of Black Chemists and Chemical Engineers *Web site*	*Daily*	Global	• College Graduates • Sciences, Engineering
NSBP.org National Society of Black Physicists *E-mail list*	*Daily*	Global	• College Graduates, Post-graduate Degree Holders • Higher Education • Sciences

Electronic

Recruiting Tool/ Type	Circulation/ Frequency	Coverage	Audience Characteristics
SACNAS.com Society for the Advancement of Chicanos and Native Americans in Science *Web site*	*Daily*	Global	• Postgraduate Degree Holders • Sciences • Spanish Language
SCEA.org Silicon Valley Chinese Engineer Association *Web site*	*Daily*	Global	• College Graduates • High-Tech • Computers/Information Technology • Chinese Language
SeniorTechs.com Senior Staff Job Information Database, The *Web site*	*Daily*	Global	• College Graduates • High-Tech • Advanced Technologies
SHPE.org Society of Hispanic Professional Engineers *Web site*	*Daily*	Global	• College Graduates • High-Tech • Engineering, Sciences • Spanish Language
SVCwireless.org Silicon Valley Chinese Wireless Technology Association *E-mail list*	*Daily*	CA	• College Graduates • High-Tech • Computers/Information Technology • Chinese Language
SWE.org Society of Women Engineers *Web site*	*Daily*	Global	• College Graduates • High-Tech • Engineering, Sciences
WITI4Hire Women in Technology *Web site*	*Daily*	Global	• College Graduates • High-Tech • Computer/Information Technology, Engineering
Woo Zone, The National Society of Black Engineers *Web site*	*Daily*	Global	• College Graduates • High-Tech • Engineering, Sciences

On-site

Recruiting Tool/ *Type*	Circulation/ *Frequency*	Coverage	Audience Characteristics
Center on Employment National Technology Institute for the Deaf *Career fair*	*Annually*	Rochester, NY	• College Students, Recent Graduates
Chinese Software Professionals Assoc. Annual Conference Chinese Software Professionals Association *Conference*	2,000 *Annually*	San Jose, CA	• College Graduates • High-Tech • Computers/Information Technology, Technology • Chinese Language
Chinese Software Professionals Assoc. Job Fair Chinese Software Professionals Association *Career fair*	2,000 *Annually*	San Jose, CA	• College Graduates • High-Tech • Computers/Information Technology, Technology • Chinese Language
NSBE National Conference National Society of Black Engineers *Conference*	*Annually*	USA	• College Graduates • High-Tech • Engineering, Sciences
SHPE Annual Convention Society of Hispanic Professional Engineers *Conference*	*Annually*	USA	• College Graduates • High-Tech • Engineering, Sciences • Spanish Language
SWE Annual Convention Society of Women Engineers *Conference*	*Annually*	USA	• College Graduates • High-Tech • Engineering, Sciences

Print

Recruiting Tool/ *Type*	Circulation/ *Frequency*	Coverage	Audience Characteristics
African American Career World Equal Opportunity Publications, Inc. *Magazine*	*Two times per year*	USA	• College Graduates • High-Tech • Computers/Information Technology, Sciences, Engineering
AWIS Magazine Association for Women in Science *Magazine*	5,000 *Quarterly*	USA	• Postgraduate Degree Holders • Sciences
Black Engineer and Information Technology Career Communications Group, Inc. *Magazine*	15,000 *Quarterly*	USA	• College Graduates • High-Tech • Sciences, Engineering
CSPA Newsletter Chinese Software Professionals Association *Newsletter*	2,000 *Quarterly*	San Jose, CA	• College Graduates • High-Tech • Advanced Technologies, Computers/Information Technology, Technology • Chinese Language
Gaea Association for Women Geoscientists *Newsletter*	1,000 *Six times per year*	USA	• Postgraduate Degree Holders • Higher Education • Sciences
Hispanic Career World Equal Opportunity Publications, Inc. *Magazine*	*Two times per year*	USA	• College Graduates • High-Tech • Computers/Information Technology, Sciences, Engineering • Spanish Language
Hispanic Engineer and Information Technology Career Communications Group, Inc. *Magazine*	15,000 *Biannually*	USA	• College Graduates • High-Tech • Sciences, Engineering • Spanish Language
Minority Engineer Equal Opportunity Publications, Inc. *Magazine/Web site*	14,067 *Three times per year*	USA	• College Graduates • High-Tech • Engineering
NACME Journal National Action Council for Minorities in Engineering, Inc. *Journal*	20,000 *Annually*	USA	• College Graduates • High-Tech • Engineering

Print

Recruiting Tool/ *Type*	Circulation/ *Frequency*	Coverage	Audience Characteristics
NSBE Bridge National Society of Black Engineers *Magazine*	140,000 *Three times per year*	USA	• College Graduates • High-Tech • Engineering, Sciences
NSBE Magazine National Society of Black Engineers *Magazine*	10,000 *Five times per year*	USA	• High School Graduates, College Graduates • High-Tech • Engineering, Sciences
SACNAS Conference Program Society for the Advancement of Chicanos and Native Americans in Science *Conference Program*	2,000 *Annually*	USA	• Computers/Information Technology, Sciences, Engineering
SHPE Magazine Society of Hispanic Professional Engineers *Magazine*	6,800 *Quarterly*	USA	• College Graduates • High-Tech • Engineering, Sciences • Spanish Language
SWE Magazine Society of Women Engineers *Magazine*	*Bimonthly*	USA	• College Graduates • High-Tech • Engineering, Sciences
Woman Engineer Equal Opportunity Publications, Inc. *Magazine/Web site*	14,126 *Three times per year*	International	• College Graduates • High-Tech • Engineering
Workforce Diversity for Engineering and IT Professionals Equal Opportunity Publications, Inc. *Magazine*	15,046 *Quarterly*	USA	• College Graduates • High-Tech • Computers/Information Technology, Sciences, Engineering

Electronic

Recruiting Tool/ Type	Circulation/ Frequency	Coverage	Audience Characteristics
50andOverboard.com Web site	Daily	Global	• High School Graduates, College Graduates
AABE American Association of Blacks in Energy Web site	Weekly	Global	• College Graduates • Energy/Natural Resources • Sciences, Engineering
Academygrad.com Midwest Military Recruiters, Inc. Web site	Daily	Global	• College Graduates
Afronet.com Afronet Web site	Daily	Global	• College Graduates
AWM Association for Women in Mathematics Web site/Newsletter	10,000 Weekly	Global	• College Graduates • Sciences
Blackworld.com Blackworld Web site	Daily	Global	• College Graduates
BlueSuitMom.com BlueSuitMom.com, Inc. Web site	Daily	Global	• College Graduates
Business-Disability.com National Business and Disability Council Web site	Daily	Global	• High School Graduates, College Graduates
Careers On-Line Disability Services, University of Minnesota Web site	Daily	Global	• College Students, Recent Graduates

Electronic

Recruiting Tool/ Type	Circulation/ Frequency	Coverage	Audience Characteristics
Cnetwork Web site	2500 members Daily	Global	• College Graduates • Chinese Language
Corporate Gray Online Competitive Edge Services, Inc. Web site/Job fair	Daily	Global	• High School Graduates, College Graduates
Destinygrp.com Destiny Group, The Web site	Daily	Global	
Diversity Employment Innovative Human Resources Solutions Web site	Daily	Global	• College Graduates
EOP.com Equal Opportunity Publications, Inc. Web site	Daily	Global	• College Graduates
iHispano.com Web site	Daily	Global	• College Graduates • Spanish Language
Inroadsinc.org INROADS, Inc. Web site	Daily	Global	
iVillage.com iVillage Web site	166,000,000 Daily	Global	• College Graduates
JMOJOBS.com Midwest Military Recruiters, Inc. Web site	Daily	Global	• College Graduates, High School Graduates, Trade/Professional School Graduates

Electronic

Recruiting Tool/ _Type_	Circulation/ _Frequency_	Coverage	Audience Characteristics
JobAccess.org Job Access _Web site_	_Daily_	Global	• College Graduates
Jobs4Women.com WWWomen, Inc. _E-mail list_	_Weekly_	San Francisco, CA	• College Graduates
LatinoWeb Job Site Latino Web _Web site_	_Daily_	Global	• Spanish Language
MilitaryHeadhunter.com Military Consulting Group _Web site_	_Daily_	Global	
NAPALSA.org National Asian Pacific American Law Student Association _Web site_	_Daily_	Global	• College Graduates • Legal
NativeAmericanJobs.com _Web site_	_Weekly_	Global	• College Graduates, High School Graduates, Trade/Professional School Graduates
NativeJobs.com Tribal Employment Newsletter _Web site_	2,000 per month _Daily_	Global	• College Graduates
NAWIC Career Center National Association of Women in Construction _Web site_	_Daily_	Global	• Trade/Professional School Graduates • Construction
NCOJobs.com Midwest Military Recruiters, Inc. _Web site_	_Daily_	Global	• College Graduates, High School Graduates, Trade/Professional School Graduates

Electronic

Recruiting Tool/ *Type*	Circulation/ *Frequency*	Coverage	Audience Characteristics
NFB Jobline National Federation for the Blind *Telephone line*		USA	• College Graduates
OpportunityBlvd.com Sacramento Observer *Web site*	*Daily*	Global	• High School Graduates, College Graduates
recruitABILITY DisabledPerson.com *Web site*	*Daily*	Global	• College Graduates
Saludos.com Saludos Hispanos *Web site*	*Daily*	Global	• College Graduates • Spanish Language
SeniorJobBank.org Senior Job Bank, Inc. *Web site*	*Daily*	Global	• High School Graduates, College Graduates
Sernational.org Ser National Jobs for Progress, Inc. *Web site*	*Daily*	Global	• Spanish Language
TAOnline.com Transition Assistance Online *Web site*	1,000,000 per month *Daily*	Global	• High School Graduates, College Graduates
Transition Bulletin Board Operation Transition *Web site*	30,000 *Daily*	Global	• High School Graduates, College Graduates
VetJobs.com *Web site*	*Daily*	Global	• High School Graduates, College Graduates

Electronic

Recruiting Tool/ Type	Circulation/ Frequency	Coverage	Audience Characteristics
Women Unlimited Job Bank Women Unlimited *Web site*	800 *Daily*	ME	• Construction
Workforce Recruitment Program for College Students with Disabilities Office of Disability Employment Policy and Department of Defense *CD-ROM*	1,000 *Annually*	USA	• College Students/Recent Graduates

On-site

Recruiting Tool/ Type	Circulation/ Frequency	Coverage	Audience Characteristics
Careers and the Disabled Career Fair Equal Opportunity Publications, Inc. *Career fair*	*Biannually*	USA	• College Graduates
Denver Indian Center Job Board Denver Indian Center *Resource center/Web site*	18,000 *Daily*	Denver, CO	• High School Graduates, College Graduates
Job Opportunities for the Blind National Federation for the Blind *Resource center*	*Daily*	USA	• College Graduates
Project Earn *Resource center*	*Daily*	USA	• Trade/Professional School Graduates, High School Graduates, College Graduates
Ser Career Fairs Ser National-Jobs for Progress, Inc. *Career fair*		USA	• Spanish Language
Title VII Diversity Career Fairs Career Fair Productions *Career fair*	*Bimonthly*	USA	• College Graduates
Women for Hire Career Fairs Women for Hire *Career fair*	*Bimonthly*	USA	• College Graduates

Print

Recruiting Tool/ *Type*	Circulation/ *Frequency*	Coverage	Audience Characteristics
Advocate, The Central Florida Advocate *Newspaper*	10,000 *Weekly*	Orlando, FL	• High School Graduates, College Graduates
Affirmative Action Register *Job Listings*	67,000 *Monthly*	USA	• High School Graduates, College Graduates
American Jewish World *Newspaper*	22,000 *Weekly*	USA	
Amsterdam News *Newspaper*	35,000 *Weekly*	New York, NY	• High School Graduates, College Graduates
Asian American Times Online Asian American Times *Magazine*	10,000 *Monthly*	Northern CA	• College Graduates
Asian Week *Newspaper*	45,716 *Weekly*	San Francisco, CA	• College Graduates
Atlanta Voice, The *Newspaper*	133,000 *Weekly*	Atlanta, GA	
Baltimore Afro-American, The Afro-American Newspaper Co., The *Newspaper*	45,000 *Weekly*	Baltimore, MD	• College Graduates
Black Chronicle, The *Newspaper*	30,088 *Weekly*	Oklahoma City, OK	• High School Graduates, College Graduates

Print

Recruiting Tool/ *Type*	Circulation/ *Frequency*	Coverage	Audience Characteristics
Black Collegian, The iMinorities, Inc. *Magazine*	*Biannually*	USA	• College Students/Recent Graduates
Black News South Carolina Media Group *Newspaper*	76,978 *Weekly*	SC	• College Graduates, High School Graduates, Trade/Professional School Graduates
Brasilian, The Brasilian Press, The *Newspaper*	45,000 *Monthly*	USA	• Portuguese Language
California Advocate, The *Newspaper*	156,039	Fresno, CA	• High School Graduates, College Graduates
Capitol Times, The *Newspaper*	*Weekly*	Austin, TX	• College Graduates
Careers and the Disabled Equal Opportunity Publications, Inc. *Magazine*	10,500 *Five times per year*	USA	• College Graduates
Carib News New York Carib News *Newspaper*	67,000 *Weekly*	New York, NY	• High School Graduates, College Graduates
Challenger Newspaper Challenger News Network *Newspaper*	5,000 *Weekly*	USA	• College Graduates
Charlotte Post *Newspaper*	23,278 *Weekly*	Charlotte, NC	• High School Graduates, College Graduates

Print

Recruiting Tool/ *Type*	Circulation/ *Frequency*	Coverage	Audience Characteristics
Cherokee Phoenix Cherokee Phoenix and Indian Advocate *Newspaper*	96,000 *Quarterly*	OK	• High School Graduates, College Graduates
Chicago Shimpo, The Chicago Shimpo/Japanese American News, The *Newspaper*	5,000 *Biweekly*	Chicago, IL	• College Graduates • Japanese Language
Chicago Standard Standard Newspapers *Newspaper*	15,000 *Weekly*	Chicago, IL	• High School Graduates, College Graduates
Chickasaw Times Chickasaw Nation *Newspaper*	17,000 *Monthly*	OK	• High School Graduates, College Graduates, Trade/Professional School Graduates
Circle News, The Circle , The *Newspaper*	20,000 *Monthly*	USA	• High School Graduates, College Graduates
Colton Courier Inland Empire Community Newspapers *Newspaper*	98,000 *Weekly*	San Bernadino, CA	• Spanish Language
Columbus Times, The Columbus Times Newspaper, The *Newspaper*	20,000 *Weekly*	Columbus, GA	
Daily Post Tribune *Newspaper*	18,500 *Weekly*	Dallas, TX	• College Graduates
El Chicano Inland Empire Community Newspapers *Newspaper*	98,000 *Weekly*	San Bernadino, CA	• Spanish Language

Recruiting Tool/ Type	Circulation/ Frequency	Coverage	Audience Characteristics
El Heraldo El Heraldo Community News *Newspaper*	22,000 *Weekly*	Southern FL	• Spanish Language
El Latino El Latino Semanal/El Latino.com *Newspaper*	36,000 *Weekly*	Palm Beach, FL	• Spanish Language
El Popular *Newspaper*	50,000 *Bimonthly*	FL, Miami-Dade, Broward, Palm Beach Counties	• Spanish Language
el Reportero *Newspaper*	16,000 *Bimonthly*	AL	• Spanish Language
El Sol de Texas *Newspaper*	80,000 *Weekly*	Dallas/Fort Worth, TX	• Spanish Language
Equal Opportunity Equal Opportunity Publications, Inc. *Magazine/Web site*	10,500 *Three times per year*	USA	• College Graduates
Florida Review Florida Review Newspaper *Newspaper*	25,000 *Bimonthly*	Miami, FL	• Portuguese Language
Florida Sentinel Florida Sentinel Bulletin *Newspaper*	22,859 *Biweekly*	Tampa, FL	• High School Graduates, College Graduates
Forward, The *Newspaper*	50,000 *Weekly*	New York, NY	• Russian Language, Yiddish Language

Print

Recruiting Tool/ Type	Circulation/ Frequency	Coverage	Audience Characteristics
Hispania News Newspaper	10,000 Weekly	Colorado Springs, CO	• Spanish Language
Houston Defender Newspaper	32,000 Weekly	Houston, TX	• College Graduates
India Abroad Newspaper	70,000 Weekly	USA	• Hindi Language
Indian Country Today Newspaper	15,000 Weekly	USA	• High School Graduates, College Graduates
Indianapolis Recorder Newspaper	13,300 Weekly	Indianapolis, IN	• High School Graduates, College Graduates
India-West India West Newspaper	30,000 Weekly	West Coast of CA	• Hindi Language
Insight News Newspaper	35,000 Weekly	Minneapolis, MN	• High School Graduates, College Graduates
Job Flash Newsletter Women Unlimited Newsletter	800 Bimonthly	ME	• Construction
La Noticia Newspaper	26,000 Weekly	Charlotte, NC	• Spanish Language

Recruiting Tool/ Type	Circulation/ Frequency	Coverage	Audience Characteristics
La Oferta Newspaper	45,000 Weekly	San Mateo, CA	• Spanish Language
La Opinion Newspaper	118,080 Daily	Southern CA	• Spanish Language
La Prensa La Prensa de Minnesota Newspaper	15,000 Weekly	St. Paul, MN	• Spanish Language
La Prensa de San Antonio Newspaper	72,000 Biweekly	San Antonio, TX	• Spanish Language
La Prensa San Diego Newspaper	30,000 Weekly	San Diego, CA	• Spanish Language
Latin American Perspectives Sage Publications Journal	700 Bimonthly	International	• College Graduates • Higher Education • Spanish Language
Lawndale News Group Newspaper	198,079 Weekly	Chicago, IL	• Spanish Language
Louisville Defender Newspaper	8,500 Weekly	Louisville, KY	• High School Graduates, College Graduates
Miami County Republic Miami County Publishing Company Newspaper	5,300 Biweekly	Miami County, KS	• High School Graduates, College Graduates

Print

Recruiting Tool/ *Type*	Circulation/ *Frequency*	Coverage	Audience Characteristics
Michigan Chronicle *Newspaper*	48,000 *Weekly*	Detroit, MI	• High School Graduates, College Graduates
Modern China Sage Publications *Journal*	650 *Quarterly*	International	• College Graduates • Chinese Language
Native American Times *Newspaper*	36,000 *Monthly*	OK	• High School Graduates, College Graduates
NAWIC Image National Association of Women in Construction *Magazine*	*Bimonthly*	USA	• Trade/Professional School Graduates • Construction
New Pittsburgh Courier *Newspaper*	*Biweekly*	Pittsburgh, PA	• College Graduates, High School Graduates, Trade/Professional School Graduates
News from Indian Country *Newspaper*	72,000 *Bimonthly*	USA	• High School Graduates, College Graduates
News from Native California *Magazine*	5,000 *Quarterly*	CA	• High School Graduates, College Graduates
Nikkei West *Newspaper*	90,000 *Biweekly*	Northern CA	• Japanese Language
NW Asian Weekly Northwest Asian Weekly *Newspaper*	25,000 *Weekly*	CA, WA, OR	

Print

Recruiting Tool/ *Type*	Circulation/ *Frequency*	Coverage	Audience Characteristics
Ojibwe Akiing *Newspaper*	5,000 *Weekly*	WI, MN, MI	• High School Graduates, College Graduates
Oklahoma Eagle *Newspaper*	35,000 *Weekly*	OK	• High School Graduates, College Graduates
Omaha Star Omaha Star, Inc., The *Newspaper*	30,000 *Weekly*	NE	• High School Graduates, College Graduates
Providence American, The Amerzine Company, The *Newspaper*	5,000 *Weekly*	RI	• High School Graduates, College Graduates
Rialto Record Inland Empire Community Newspapers *Newspaper*	98,000 *Weekly*	San Bernadino, CA	• Spanish Language
Sacramento Observer *Newspaper*	49,600 *Weekly*	Sacramento, CA	• High School Graduates, College Graduates
San Francisco Bay View *Newspaper*	20,000 *Weekly*	San Francisco, CA	• College Graduates
Sing Tao Newspaper Sing Tao Newspapers New York Ltd. *Newspaper*	55,000 *Daily*	New York, NY	• Chinese Language
Skanner, The Skanner News Group, The *Newspaper*	75,000 *Weekly*	Portland, OR; Seattle, WA	• High School Graduates, College Graduates

GENERAL RECRUITMENT

Print

Recruiting Tool/ *Type*	Circulation/ *Frequency*	Coverage	Audience Characteristics
South Suburban Standard Standard Newspapers *Newspaper*	25,000 *Weekly*	South Suburbs, Chicago IL	• High School Graduates, College Graduates
Southwest Digest Newspaper Southwest Digest *Newspaper*	20,000 *Weekly*	West TX, Eastern NM	• High School Graduates, College Graduates
Speakin' Out News *Newspaper*	26,000 *Weekly*	Huntsville, Decatur AL; Tennessee Valley	• College Graduates
Spokesman-Recorder, The *Newspaper*	26,000 *Weekly*	Minneapolis, MN	• High School Graduates, College Graduates
St. Louis American *Newspaper*	65,000 *Weekly*	St. Louis, MO	• College Graduates
St. Louis Chinese American News *Newspaper*	5,000 *Weekly*	St. Louis, MO	• Chinese Language
St. Louis Sentinel St. Louis Sentinel Newspaper, The *Newspaper*	100,000 *Weekly*	St. Louis, MO	
Sun Reporter Sun Publishing Company *Newspaper*	11,000 *Weekly*	Northern CA	
Title VII Diversity Career Fair Exhibitor Guide Career Fair Productions *Exhibitor's Guide*	*Bimonthly*	USA	• College Graduates

GENERAL RECRUITMENT

Print

Recruiting Tool/ Type	Circulation/ Frequency	Coverage	Audience Characteristics
Tri-State Defender Newspaper	Weekly	Memphis, TN	• High School Graduates, College Graduates
Twin Visions Newspaper	30,000 Weekly	Newark, NJ	• High School Graduates, College Graduates
Urban Spectrum, The Newspaper	60,000 Monthly	Denver, CO	• College Graduates
Washington Afro-American, The Afro-American Newspaper Co., The Newspaper	45,000 Weekly	Washington, DC	• College Graduates

MANAGERS AND EXECUTIVES

Electronic

Recruiting Tool/ Type	Circulation/ Frequency	Coverage	Audience Characteristics
FWA.org Financial Women's Association of New York *Web site*	*Monthly*	Global	• Postgraduate Degree Holders • Finance
NAAAHR.org National Association of African Americans in Human Resources *Web site*	*Weekly*	Global	• College Graduates • Human Resources
National Black MBA Job Posting System National Black MBA Association *Web site*	*Daily*	Global	• Postgraduate Degree Holders
NHCC-HQ.org National Hispanic Corporate Council *Web site*	*Daily*	Global	• College Graduates • Spanish Language
NSHMBA.org National Society of Hispanic MBAs *Web site*	*Daily*	Global	• Postgraduate Degree Holders • Spanish Language
Womens Executive Network *Web site*	1,000,000 *Daily*	Global	• College Graduates

On-site

Recruiting Tool/ *Type*	Circulation/ *Frequency*	Coverage	Audience Characteristics
ABWA National Convention Career Fair American Business Women's Association *Career fair*	70,000 *Annually*	USA	• College Graduates
Hispanic MBA Career Fairs National Society of Hispanic MBAs *Career fair*	*Monthly*	USA	• College Graduates
NAHFE Annual Conference National Association of Hispanic Federal Executives *Conference*	*Annually*	USA	• Government • Spanish Language
National Black MBA Career Fairs National Black MBA Association *Career fair*	*Monthly*	USA	• College Graduates
National Conference National Black MBA Association *Conference*	*Annually*	USA	• Postgraduate Degree Holders

Print

Recruiting Tool/ Type	Circulation/ Frequency	Coverage	Audience Characteristics
Arab American News, The Newspaper	22,000 Weekly	Detroit, MI	• Arabic Language
Black Enterprise Magazine Earl Graves Publishing Co. Inc. Magazine	475,000 Monthly	USA	• College Graduates
Black MBA Magazine National Black MBA Association Magazine	Quarterly	USA	• Postgraduate Degree Holders
Bottom Line, The National Society of Hispanic MBAs Newsletter	5,000 Monthly	USA	• Postgraduate Degree Holders • Spanish Language
FWA News Financial Women's Association of New York Newsletter	1,100 Monthly	USA	• Postgraduate Degree Holders • Finance
Hispanic Business Magazine Magazine	215,000 Monthly	USA	• College Graduates • Spanish Language
Hispanic Magazine Hispanic Publishing Corporation Magazine	250,000 Monthly	USA	• College Graduates • Spanish Language
Hispanic MBA National Society of Hispanic MBAs Magazine	15,000 Biannually	USA	• Postgraduate Degree Holders • Spanish Language
Jewish Chronicle, The Newspaper	14,000 Weekly	Pittsburgh, PA	• College Graduates

Print

Recruiting Tool/ Type	Circulation/ Frequency	Coverage	Audience Characteristics
Women In Business American Business Women's Association *Magazine*	70,000 *Bimonthly*	USA	• College Graduates

Electronic

Recruiting Tool/ Type	Circulation/ Frequency	Coverage	Audience Characteristics
AAHCPA.org American Association of Hispanic CPAs Web site	Daily	Global	• College Graduates • Accounting • Spanish Language
AAIP Association of American Indian Physicians Web site	Daily	Global	• MD, PhD • Health Care • Medical
AAMA Asian American Manufacturers Association Web site	Daily	Global	• College Graduates • Manufacturing
AAUW.org American Association of University Women Web site	1,894,050 Weekly	Global	• College Graduates • Higher Education
ABC Association of Black Cardiologists Web site	Daily	Global	• MD, PhD • Health Care • Medical
Advancing Women Network Advancing Women Electronic newsletter	Daily	Global	• College Graduates
AdvancingWomen.com Advancing Women Web site	Daily	Global	• College Graduates
Africareers.com Diversity Village Inc. Web site	Daily	Global	• College Graduates
Asiancareers.com Diversity Village Inc. Web site	Daily	Global	• College Graduates

Electronic

Recruiting Tool/ *Type*	Circulation/ *Frequency*	Coverage	Audience Characteristics
ASWA American Society of Women Accountants *Web site*	15,000 *Daily*	Global	• Accounting, Finance
AWIP Association of Professional Insurance Women *Web site*	*Daily*	Global	• College Graduates • Insurance
AWMI Association of Women in the Metal Industries *Web site*	*Daily*	Global	• Industrial
AWP Association of Women Professionals *Web site*	*Daily*	Global	• College Graduates
AWRT CareerLine American Women in Radio and Television *Fax-on-demand list*	*Biweekly*	USA	• College Graduates • Communications
AWSCPA American Society of Women CPAs *Web site*	*Daily*	Global	• Accounting
BIGnet.org Blacks in Government *Web site*	*Weekly*	Global	• Government
BlackEnterprise.com Black Enterprise Career Channel *Web site*	*Daily*	Global	
BlackStocks.com Strategic Interactive Media, Inc. *Web site*	*Daily*	Global	• College Graduates • Investment

P R O F E S S I O N A L S

Electronic

Recruiting Tool/ Type	Circulation/ Frequency	Coverage	Audience Characteristics
BlackVoices.com Web site	600,000 Daily	Global	• College Graduates
Boston Chapter of NAAAP National Association of Asian American Professionals Web site	Monthly	Global	• College Graduates
Career Opportunity and Exchange National Association of Hispanic Journalists Web site	Weekly	Global	• College Graduates • Communications • Spanish Language
Careerwoman2000.com Diversity Village Inc. Web site	Daily	Global	• College Graduates
CareerWomen.com Career Exposure Web site	Daily	Global	• College Graduates
CCNMA California Chicano News Media Association Web site	Daily	Global	• Communications • Spanish Language
DiversiLink Innovative Human Resources Solutions Web site	Daily	Global	• College Graduates
DiversityRecruiting.com Richard Clarke & Associates, Inc. Web site	Daily	Global	• College Graduates
HACE Candidate Referral Service Hispanic Alliance for Career Enhancement Web site	4,000 Weekly	Global	• College Graduates • Spanish Language

P R O F E S S I O N A L S

Electronic

Recruiting Tool/ *Type*	Circulation/ *Frequency*	Coverage	Audience Characteristics
HACE-USA.ORG Hispanic Alliance for Career Enhancement *Web site*	*Daily*	Global	• College Graduates • Spanish Language
HireDiversity.com Hispanic Business.com *Web site*	*Daily*	Global	• College Graduates
Hispanicareers.com Diversity Village Inc. *Web site*	*Daily*	Global	• College Graduates • Spanish Language
HispanicHealth.org National Coalition of Hispanic Health and Human Service Organizations *Web site*	*Daily*	Global	• College Graduates • Health Care • Medical, Social Services • Spanish Language
HispanicOnline.com Hispanic Publishing Corporation *Web site*	*Daily*	Global	• College Graduates • Spanish Language
HNBA.com Hispanic National Bar Association *Web site*	*Monthly*	Global	• Postgraduate Degree Holders • Legal • Spanish Language
Iamable.net Diversity Village Inc. *Web site*	*Daily*	Global	• College Graduates
IMDiversity.com iMinorities, Inc. *Web site*	*Daily*	Global	• College Graduates
LatPro.com LatPro, Inc. *Web site*	200,000 *Daily*	Global	• College Graduates • Spanish Language, Portuguese Language

Electronic

Recruiting Tool/ *Type*	Circulation/ *Frequency*	Coverage	Audience Characteristics
Member Listserv Asian American Journalist Association *E-mail list*	112,756 *Weekly*	Global	• College Graduates • Communications
NABA Corporate Career Center National Association of Black Accountants *Web site*	*Daily*	Global	• College Graduates • Accounting
NABJobs National Association of Black Journalists *Web site*	*Daily*	Global	• College Graduates • Communications
NAIW.org National Association of Insurance Women *Web site*	*Daily*	Global	• College Graduates • Insurance
NAJA Native American Journalist Association *Web site*	*Weekly*	Global	• College Graduates • Communications
NAPMW National Association of Professional Mortgage Women *Web site*	*Daily*	Global	• Finance
NASBE.org National Alliance of Black School Educators *Web site*	*Daily*	Global	• College Graduates • Higher Education
NASPHQ.com National Association of Securities Professionals *Web site*	*Daily*	Global	• College Graduates • Investment

Electronic

Recruiting Tool/ *Type*	Circulation/ *Frequency*	Coverage	Audience Characteristics
National Association of Negro Business and Professional Womens Clubs Job Line National Association of Negro Business and Professional Women's Clubs *Phone line*	*Weekly*	USA	
NBPRS.com National Black Public Relations Society *Web site*	*Weekly*	Global	• College Graduates • Communications
NDNJB National Diversity Newspaper Job Bank, The *Web site*	80,924 *Daily*	Global	• College Graduates • Communications
Nemnet National Employment Minority Network, The *E-mail list*	2,000 *Weekly*	Global	• College Graduates, College Students, Recent Graduates
Nemnet National Employment Minority Network, The *Web site*	*Daily*	Global	• College Graduates, College Students, Recent Graduates
NetNoir.com Chapman Network Inc. *Web site*	*Daily*	Global	• College Graduates
NHBA.org National Hispanic Business Association *Web site*	*Daily*	Global	• College Graduates • Spanish Language
NOMA.net National Organization of Minority Architects *Web site*	*Daily*	Global	• College Graduates • Architecture

Electronic

Recruiting Tool/ *Type*	Circulation/ *Frequency*	Coverage	Audience Characteristics
PICKDiversity.com PICKDiversity *Web site*	*Daily*	Global	• College Graduates
TBWCareers.com Black World Today, The *Web site*	*Daily*	Global	
Womcom.org Association for Women in Communications *Web site*	*Daily*	Global	• College Graduates • Communications
Women in Natural Resources *Web site*	*Daily*	Global	• College Graduates • Energy/Natural Resources • Sciences
WorkplaceDiversity.com *Web site*	*Daily*	Global	• College Graduates

On-site

Recruiting Tool/ *Type*	Circulation/ *Frequency*	Coverage	Audience Characteristics
AAHCPA Career Fair/Expo American Association of Hispanic CPAs *Career fair*	*Annually*	USA	• College Graduates • Accounting • Spanish Language
BlackVoices Career Fairs BlackVoicescom. *Career fair*	600,000 *Quarterly*	USA	• College Graduates
HACE Career Conference Hispanic Alliance for Career Enhancement *Conference*	*Yearly*	USA	• College Graduates • Spanish Language
Hire Diversity Career Fairs HireDiversity.com *Career fair*	*Biannually*	USA	• College Graduates
Latino Law Student Job Fair Hispanic National Bar Association *Career fair*	*Annually*	USA	• Postgraduate Degree Holders • Legal • Spanish Language
Minority Networking Night Columbus Times Newspaper, The *Conference*	*Monthly*	Columbus, GA	
NAACP Career Fairs NAACP - National Association for the Advancement of Colored People *Career fair*	4,000 *Monthly*	USA	• College Graduates, Postgraduate Degree Holders
National Association of Hispanic Nurses Annual Conference National Association of Hispanic Nurses *Conference*	*Annually*	USA	• College Graduates • Health Care • Medical • Spanish Language
NBNA Conference National Black Nurses Association *Conference*	*Annually*	USA	• College Graduates • Health Care • Medical

PROFESSIONALS

On-site

Recruiting Tool/ *Type*	Circulation/ *Frequency*	Coverage	Audience Characteristics

Nemnet
National Employment
  Minority Network, The
Career fair
	Varied	USA	• College Graduates, College
			  Students, Recent Graduates

PICKDiversity Career Fair PICKDiversity *Career fair*	*Quarterly*	USA	• College Graduates

Print

Recruiting Tool/ Type	Circulation/ Frequency	Coverage	Audience Characteristics
AAUW Outlook American Association of University Women *Magazine*	150,000 *Quarterly*	USA	• College Graduates • Higher Education
Black Issues in Higher Education Black Issues in Higher Education *Magazine*	40,000 *Biweekly*	USA	• College Graduates • Higher Education
Black MBA Magazine iMinorities, Inc. *Magazine*	29,275 *Biannually*	USA	• Postgraduate Degree Holders
Black Perspective, The E. M. Publishing Enterprises *Magazine*	7,500 *Quarterly*	USA	• College Graduates
BVQ Magazine BlackVoices.com *Magazine*	600,000 *Quarterly*	USA	• College Graduates
Contempora Magazine *Magazine*	36,000 *Bimonthly*	Nashville, TN	• College Graduates
Crisis Magazine, The NAACP - National Association for the Advancement of Colored People *Magazine*	250,000 *Bimonthly*	USA	• College Graduates
Dos Mundos *Newspaper*	70,000 *Biweekly*	Kansas City, MO	• Spanish Language
Hispanic Journal of Behavioral Sciences Sage Publications *Journal*	500 *Quarterly*	International	• College Graduates • Higher Education • Spanish Language

Print

Recruiting Tool/ *Type*	Circulation/ *Frequency*	Coverage	Audience Characteristics
Hispanic Link Weekly Report Hispanic Link News Service *Newsletter*	18,000 *Weekly*	USA	• College Graduates • Spanish Language
Hispanic Nurses Unnamed Journal National Association of Hispanic Nurses *Journal*	*Quarterly*	USA	• College Graduates • Health Care • Medical • Spanish Language
Hispanic Today E. M. Publishing Enterprises *Magazine*	7,500 *Quarterly*	USA	• College Graduates • Spanish Language
Jewish Business Quarterly E. M. Publishing Enterprises *Magazine*	7,500 *Quarterly*	USA	• College Graduates
Journal of African American Men Transaction Publishers *Journal*	400 *Quarterly*	USA	• College Graduates • Higher Education
Journal of American Ethnic History Transaction Publishers *Journal*	*Quarterly*	International	• College Graduates • Higher Education
Journal of Black Psychology Sage Publications *Journal*	1,000 *Quarterly*	International	• College Graduates
Journal of Black Studies Sage Publications *Journal*	800 *Bimonthly*	International	• College Graduates • Higher Education
Journal of the National Black Nurses Association National Black Nurses Association *Journal*	8,500 *Biannually*	USA	• College Graduates • Health Care • Medical

Print

Recruiting Tool/ *Type*	Circulation/ *Frequency*	Coverage	Audience Characteristics
Milwaukee Times, The *Newspaper*	15,000 *Weekly*	Milwaukee, WI	
NBNA Newsletter National Black Nurses Association *Newsletter*	6,000 *Quarterly*	USA	• College Graduates • Health Care • Medical
Network International Women's Writing Guild *Newsletter*	4,000 *Bimonthly*	International	• College Graduates • Communications
PICKDiversity Program **Magazine** PICKDiversity *Magazine*	*Quarterly*	USA	• College Graduates
Review of Black Political **Economy** Transaction Publishers *Journal*	800 *Quarterly*	USA	• College Graduates • Higher Education
Tennessee Tribune *Newspaper*	45,000 *Weekly*	Nashville, TN	
Veteran's Enterprise E. M. Publishing Enterprises *Magazine*	7,500 *Quarterly*	USA	• College Graduates
Veteran's Vision E. M. Publishing Enterprises *Magazine*	7,500 *Quarterly*	USA	• College Graduates
Washington Informer, The Washington Informer Newspaper, The *Newspaper*	27,000 *Weekly*	Washington, DC	• College Graduates

Print

Recruiting Tool/ *Type*	Circulation/ *Frequency*	Coverage	Audience Characteristics
Women in Natural Resources Job Flyer Women in Natural Resources *Job Listings*	*Monthly*	USA	• College Graduates • Energy/Natural Resources • Sciences
Women in Natural Resources Journal Women in Natural Resources *Journal*	*Quarterly*	USA	• College Graduates • Energy/Natural Resources • Sciences

Recruiting Tools in Alphabetical Order

50andOverboard.com

www.50andoverboard.com
info@50andoverboard.com

TYPE/ FREQUENCY: Web site/ Daily

DESCRIPTION:
Web site targeted to employees 50 and over.

COVERAGE: Global

RATES:
Free.

RECRUITING SECTION: General Recruitment

AUDIENCE CHARACTERISTICS:
• High School Graduates, College Graduates

ADVERTISING CONTACT:
info@50andoverboard.com

AABE

American Association of Blacks in Energy
927 15th St. NW, #200
Washington, DC 20005
PH: (202) 371-9530
FAX: (202) 371-9218
www.aabe.org
aabe@aabe.org

TYPE/ FREQUENCY: Web site/ Weekly

DESCRIPTION:
Black energy professionals.

COVERAGE: Global

RATES:
Employer entering data: 1 year: $4,600, 1/2 year unlimited: $2,850; single 4-day posting: $150; each additional 45-day posting: $100 (up to 5).

RECRUITING SECTION: General Recruitment

AUDIENCE CHARACTERISTICS:
• College Graduates
• Energy/ Natural Resources
• Sciences, Engineering

ADVERTISING CONTACT:
Jobs Board
PH: (202) 371-9530
FAX: (202) 371-9218
aabe@aabe.org

AAHCPA Career Fair/Expo

American Association of Hispanic CPAs
611 W. 6th St., #2500
Los Angeles, CA 90048
PH: (213) 236-2703
FAX: (213) 236-2700
www.aahcpa.org
aahcpaed@netscape.net

TYPE/ FREQUENCY: Career fair/ Annually

DESCRIPTION:
Professional association supporting Hispanic CPAs and students. The annual convention has a career fair and expo.

COVERAGE: USA

RATES:
Sponsorship levels start at Patron $2,500 (includes booth at career fair).

RECRUITING SECTION: Professionals

AUDIENCE CHARACTERISTICS:
• College Graduates
• Accounting
• Spanish Language

ADVERTISING CONTACT:
Opportunities
PH: (213) 236-2703
FAX: (213) 236-2700
aahcpaed@netscape.net

AAHCPA.org

American Association of Hispanic CPAs
611 W. 6th St., #2500
Los Angeles, CA 90048
PH: (213) 236-2703
FAX: (213) 236-2700
www.aahcpa.org
aahcpaed@netscape.net

TYPE/ FREQUENCY: Web site/ Daily

DESCRIPTION:
Hispanic CPA professional organization.

COVERAGE: Global

RATES:
$250 per month per job.

RECRUITING SECTION: Professionals

AUDIENCE CHARACTERISTICS:
• College Graduates
• Accounting
• Spanish Language

ADVERTISING CONTACT:
Opportunities
PH: (213) 236-2703
FAX: (213) 236-2700
aahcpaed@netscape.net

AAIP

Association of American Indian Physicians
1225 Sovereign Row, #103
Oklahoma City, OK 73108
PH: (405) 946-7972
FAX: (405) 946-7651
www.aaip.com
aaip@aaip.com

TYPE/ FREQUENCY: Web site/ Daily

DESCRIPTION:
AAIP is dedicated to pursuing excellence in Native American health care by promoting education in the medical disciplines, honoring traditional healing practices, and restoring the balance of mind, body, and spirit.

COVERAGE: Global

RATES:
Classifieds: $25 for 3 months; $50 for 6 months.

RECRUITING SECTION: Professionals

AUDIENCE CHARACTERISTICS:
• MD, PhD
• Health Care
• Medical

ADVERTISING CONTACT:
Classifieds
PH: (405) 946-7072
FAX: (405) 946-7651
aaip@aaip.com

AAMA

Asian American Manufacturers Association
1270 Oakmead Pkwy., #201
Sunnyvale, CA 94085
PH: (408) 736-2554
FAX: (408) 736-2589
www.aamasv.com
aama@aamasv.com

TYPE/ FREQUENCY: Web site/ Daily

DESCRIPTION:
Manufacturing association.

COVERAGE: Global

RATES:
Job listings are for member companies only; memberships are $450 and $1,200 levels.

RECRUITING SECTION: Professionals

AUDIENCE CHARACTERISTICS:
• College Graduates
• Manufacturing

ADVERTISING CONTACT:
Job Bank
PH: (408) 736-2554
FAX: (408) 736-2589
aama@aamasv.com

AAUW Outlook

American Association of University Women
1111 16th St. NW
Washington, DC 20036
PH: (202) 785-7774
FAX: (202) 872-1425
www.aauw.org
ads@aauw.org

TYPE/ FREQUENCY: Magazine/ Quarterly

DESCRIPTION:
The official magazine of AAUW.

CIRCULATION/ AUDITED BY: 150,000

COVERAGE: USA

RATES:
$125 per column inch.

RECRUITING SECTION: Professionals

AUDIENCE CHARACTERISTICS:
- College Graduates
- Higher Education

ADVERTISING CONTACT:
Advertising
PH: (202) 728-7606
FAX: (202) 872-1425
ads@aauw.org

AAUW.org

American Association of University Women
1111 16th St. NW
Washington, DC 20036
PH: (202) 785-7774
FAX: (202) 872-1425
www.aauw.org
ads@aauw.org

TYPE/ FREQUENCY: Web site/ Weekly

DESCRIPTION:
The official web site of AAUW; job market feature.

CIRCULATION/ AUDITED BY: 1,894,050

COVERAGE: Global

RATES:
$5 per word per month.

RECRUITING SECTION: Professionals

AUDIENCE CHARACTERISTICS:
- College Graduates
- Higher Education

ADVERTISING CONTACT:
Advertising
PH: (202) 728-7606
FAX: (202) 872-1425
ads@aauw.org

ABC

Association of Black Cardiologists
6849-B2 Peachtree Dunwoody Rd. NE
Atlanta, GA 30328
PH: (675) 302-4ABC
FAX: (678) 302-4223
www.abcardio.org

TYPE/ FREQUENCY: Web site/ Daily

DESCRIPTION:
The ABC is a not-for-profit volunteer organization of 700 African American cardiologists and medical professionals that is fully accredited by the ACCME.

COVERAGE: Global

RATES:
Currently free.

RECRUITING SECTION: Professionals

AUDIENCE CHARACTERISTICS:
- MD, PhD
- Health Care
- Medical

ADVERTISING CONTACT:
PH: (678) 302-4ABC
FAX: (678) 302-4223

ABWA National Convention Career Fair

American Business Women's Association
9100 Ward Pkwy.
PO Box 8728
Kansas City, MO 64114-0728
PH: (816) 361-6621
FAX: (816) 361-4991
www.abwa.org
wmabrey@abwa.org

TYPE/ FREQUENCY: Career fair/ Annually

DESCRIPTION:
Career fair held in conjunction with ABWA national convention.

CIRCULATION/ AUDITED BY: 70,000

COVERAGE: USA

RATES:
Contact for rates.

RECRUITING SECTION: Managers and Executives

AUDIENCE CHARACTERISTICS:
- College Graduates

ADVERTISING CONTACT:
Wendy Mabrey
Corporate Sponsorship
PH: (816) 361-6621 ext. 260
FAX: (816) 361-4991
wmabrey@abwa.org

Academygrad.com

Midwest Military Recruiters, Inc.
1396 Windburn Dr.
Marietta, GA 30066
PH: (770) 579-4687
FAX: (770) 579-4690
www.academygrad.com
gshook@mediaone.net

TYPE/ FREQUENCY: Web site/ Daily

DESCRIPTION:
Web site targets military personnel who graduated from military academies.

COVERAGE: Global

RATES:
Basic web site job posting: $75 per ad per month.

RECRUITING SECTION: General Recruitment

AUDIENCE CHARACTERISTICS:
• College Graduates

ADVERTISING CONTACT:
Greg Shook
PH: (770) 579-4687
FAX: (770) 579-4690
gshook@mediaone.net

Advancing Women Network

Advancing Women
3463 Magic Dr.
San Antonio, TX 78229
PH: (210) 582-5835
FAX: (210) 582-5837
www.advancingwomen.com

TYPE/ FREQUENCY: Electronic newsletter/ Daily

DESCRIPTION:
Targets women professionals; winner of Lycos top 5% award; daily e-zine.

COVERAGE: Global

RATES:
Contact for rates.

RECRUITING SECTION: Professionals

AUDIENCE CHARACTERISTICS:
• College Graduates

ADVERTISING CONTACT:
Gretchen Glasscock
PH: (210) 582-5835
FAX: (210) 582-5837
ads@advancingwomen.com

AdvancingWomen.com

Advancing Women
3463 Magic Dr.
San Antonio, TX 78229
PH: (210) 582-5835
FAX: (210) 582-5837
www.advancingwomen.com

TYPE/ FREQUENCY: Web site/ Daily

DESCRIPTION:
Targets women professionals; winner of Lycos top 5% award; career center powered by HeadHunter.net.

COVERAGE: Global

RATES:
$100 per job per month; other packages available.

RECRUITING SECTION: Professionals

AUDIENCE CHARACTERISTICS:
• College Graduates

ADVERTISING CONTACT:
HeadHunter.net
PH: (877) 235-8978

The Advocate

Central Florida Advocate
218 S. Lime Ave.
Orlando, FL 32805
PH: (407) 648-1162
FAX: (407) 649-8702

TYPE/ FREQUENCY: Newspaper/ Weekly

DESCRIPTION:
African American community news.

CIRCULATION/ AUDITED BY: 10,000

COVERAGE: Orlando, FL

RATES:
$8.75 per column inch.

RECRUITING SECTION: General Recruitment

AUDIENCE CHARACTERISTICS:
• High School Graduates, College Graduates

ADVERTISING CONTACT:
Derrick Drake
Advertising
PH: (407) 648-1162
cfa_ads@hotmail.com

Affirmative Action Register

8356 Olive Blvd.
St. Louis, MO 63132
PH: (800) 537-0655
FAX: (314) 997-1788
www.aar-eeo.com
aareeo@concentric.net

TYPE/ FREQUENCY: Job Listings/ Monthly

DESCRIPTION:
The national EEO recruitment publication directed to females, minorities, veterans, and disabled employment candidates.

CIRCULATION/ AUDITED BY: 67,000/ CAS

COVERAGE: USA

RATES:
1/6 page $425; 1/2 page $1,200.

RECRUITING SECTION: General Recruitment

AUDIENCE CHARACTERISTICS:
• High School Graduates, College Graduates

ADVERTISING CONTACT:
PH: (800) 537-0655
FAX: (314) 997-1788
aareeo@concentric.net

African American Career World

Equal Opportunity Publications, Inc.
445 Broad Hollow Rd., #425
Melville, NY 11747
PH: (631) 421-9421
FAX: (631) 421-0359
www.eop.com
info@eop.com

TYPE/ FREQUENCY: Magazine/ Two times per year

DESCRIPTION:
Serves as a link between engineering student and professionals and high-tech companies that seek such technical specialists.

COVERAGE: USA

RATES:
$250 per month per magazine for online editions; call for print rates.

RECRUITING SECTION: Advanced Technologies

AUDIENCE CHARACTERISTICS:
• College Graduates
• High-Tech
• Computers/Information Technology, Sciences, Engineering

ADVERTISING CONTACT:
Advertising
PH: (631) 421-9421
FAX: (631) 421-0359
info@eop.com

Africareers.com

Diversity Village Inc.
287 E. 6th St.
#200
St. Paul, MN 55105
PH: (651) 224-0330
FAX: (651) 224-0740
www.africareers.com

TYPE/ FREQUENCY: Web site/ Daily

DESCRIPTION:
Web site providing recruitment and career resources to African Americans.

COVERAGE: Global

RATES:
Contact for rates.

RECRUITING SECTION: Professionals

AUDIENCE CHARACTERISTICS:
• College Graduates

ADVERTISING CONTACT:
Omar Salas
Sales
PH: (651) 224-0330
FAX: (651) 224-0740

Afronet.com

Afronet
PO Box 43631
Los Angeles, CA 90043
PH: (334) 341-1560
FAX: (310) 313-2438
www.afronet.com
afronet@afronet.com

TYPE/ FREQUENCY: Web site/ Daily

DESCRIPTION:
An Internet site devoted to the African American community. Career Center is powered by HotJobs.

COVERAGE: Global

RATES:
$220 per job per month.

RECRUITING SECTION: General Recruitment

AUDIENCE CHARACTERISTICS:
• College Graduates

ADVERTISING CONTACT:
Willie Atterberry
PH: (334) 341-1560
FAX: (310) 313-2438

AISES.com

American Indian Science and Engineering Society
PO Box 9828
Albuquerque, NM 87119-9828
PH: (505) 765-1052
FAX: (505) 765-5608
www.aises.org

TYPE/ FREQUENCY: Web site/ Daily

DESCRIPTION:
Official web site of the American Indian Science and Engineering Society, which promotes the advancement of Native Americans in those fields.

COVERAGE: Global

RATES:
For profit text plus link to company web site $250; nonprofit $125 (per job).

RECRUITING SECTION: Advanced Technologies

AUDIENCE CHARACTERISTICS:
• College Graduates
• High-Tech
• Engineering, Sciences

ADVERTISING CONTACT:
Job Postings
PH: (505) 765-1052
FAX: (505) 765-5608

American Jewish World

4509 Minnetonka Blvd.
Minneapolis, MN 55416
PH: (952) 259-5280
FAX: (952) 920-6205
amjewish@isd.net

TYPE/ FREQUENCY: Newspaper/ Weekly

DESCRIPTION:
Directed toward middle aged Jewish audience with high educational and financial demographics.

CIRCULATION/ AUDITED BY: 22,000

COVERAGE: USA

RATES:
$12 for first 5 lines, $2 each additional line.

RECRUITING SECTION: General Recruitment

ADVERTISING CONTACT:
Classifieds
PH: (952) 259-5280
FAX: (952) 920-6205
amjewish@isd.net

Amsterdam News

2340 Frederick Douglass Blvd.
New York, NY 10027
PH: (212) 932-7400
FAX: (212) 222-3842

TYPE/ FREQUENCY: Newspaper/ Weekly

DESCRIPTION:
America's largest Black-oriented weekly newspaper.

CIRCULATION/ AUDITED BY: 35,000/ ABC

COVERAGE: New York, NY

RATES:
$5.15 per line minimum 4 lines; career and business $74.25 per column inch.

RECRUITING SECTION: General Recruitment

AUDIENCE CHARACTERISTICS:
• High School Graduates, College Graduates

ADVERTISING CONTACT:
Classifieds
PH: (212) 932-7440
FAX: (212) 932-7431

The Arab American News

5706 Chase Rd.
Dearborn, MI 48126
PH: (313) 582-4888
FAX: (313) 582-7870
www.arabamericannews.com
osiblani@aol.com

TYPE/ FREQUENCY: Newspaper/ Weekly

DESCRIPTION:
Independent newspaper for the Arab American community in Detroit.

CIRCULATION/ AUDITED BY: 22,000

COVERAGE: Detroit, MI

RATES:
Classified rate: $1 per word.

RECRUITING SECTION: Managers and Executives

AUDIENCE CHARACTERISTICS:
• Arabic Language

ADVERTISING CONTACT:
Nizar Matta
PH: (313) 582-4888
FAX: (313) 582-7870

Asian American Times Online

Asian American Times
Serramonte del Rey, #226
699 Serramonte Blvd.
Dale City, CA 94015-4132
PH: (650) 992-2708
FAX: (408) 369-1701
www.aatimes.com
editor@aatimes.com

TYPE/ FREQUENCY: Magazine/ Monthly

DESCRIPTION:
Asian American monthly review.

CIRCULATION/ AUDITED BY: 10,000

COVERAGE: Northern CA

RATES:
$75 for online classified listing (1 time); $50 for print (1 time) per 6 lines.

RECRUITING SECTION: General Recruitment

AUDIENCE CHARACTERISTICS:
• College Graduates

ADVERTISING CONTACT:
Classifieds
PH: (650) 992-2708
FAX: (408) 369-1701
editor@aatimes.com

Asian Week

809 Sacramento St.
San Francisco, CA 94108
PH: (415) 397-0220
FAX: (415) 397-7258
www.asianweek.com
asianweek@asianweek.com

TYPE/ FREQUENCY: Newspaper/ Weekly

DESCRIPTION:
Asian American newspaper in English targeting second and third generation Asian Americans and their families who are not reached by in-language papers.

CIRCULATION/ AUDITED BY: 45,716/ VAC

COVERAGE: San Francisco , CA

RATES:
$40 per column inch.

RECRUITING SECTION: General Recruitment

AUDIENCE CHARACTERISTICS:
• College Graduates

ADVERTISING CONTACT:
V. Womack
Advertising
PH: (415) 397-0220 ext. 15
FAX: (415) 397-3080
vwomack@asianweek.com

Asiancareers.com

Diversity Village Inc.
287 E. 6th St., #200
St. Paul, MN 55105
PH: (651) 224-0330
FAX: (651) 224-0740
www.asiancareers.com

TYPE/ FREQUENCY: Web site/ Daily

DESCRIPTION:
Web site providing recruitment and career resources to Asian Americans.

COVERAGE: Global

RATES:
Contact for rates.

RECRUITING SECTION: Professionals

AUDIENCE CHARACTERISTICS:
• College Graduates

ADVERTISING CONTACT:
Omar Salas
Sales
PH: (651) 224-0330
FAX: (651) 224-0740

ASWA

American Society of Women Accountants
National Headquarters
1595 Spring Hill Rd.
#330
Vienna, VA 22182
PH: (800) 326-2163
FAX: (703) 506-3266
www.aswa.org
aswa@aswa.org

TYPE/ FREQUENCY: Web site/ Daily

DESCRIPTION:
A professional organization whose purpose is to advance the interest of women in all fields of accounting and finance. Has 100 chapters and approximately 6,000 members.

CIRCULATION/ AUDITED BY: 15,000

COVERAGE: Global

RATES:
$150 per month for the first 50 words, $2 per word for additional copy; a link and logo added is additional $50 per item per month; sponsorship of the Employment Opportunities page is $350 per month and will include a listing, link, and banner ad.

RECRUITING SECTION: Professionals

AUDIENCE CHARACTERISTICS:
• Accounting, Finance

ADVERTISING CONTACT:
Employment Opportunities
PH: (703) 506-3265
FAX: (703) 506-3266
aswa@aswa.org

The Atlanta Voice

633 Pryor St.
PO Box 2123
Atlanta, GA 30312
PH: (404) 524-6426
FAX: (770) 263-7003
www.theatlantavoice.com
ronshook@mediaone.net

TYPE/ FREQUENCY: Newspaper/ Weekly

DESCRIPTION:
African American community news.

CIRCULATION/ AUDITED BY: 133,000/ CPVS

COVERAGE: Atlanta, GA

RATES:
Free for 30 days.

RECRUITING SECTION: General Recruitment

ADVERTISING CONTACT:
Ron Shook
PH: (404) 524-6426
FAX: (770) 263-7003
ronshook@mediaone.net

AWG E-Mail News

Association for Women Geoscientists
University of Illinois
Dept. of Geology
1301 W. Green St.
Urbana, IL 61801
PH: (217) 367-5916
www.awg.org
ads@awg.org

TYPE/ FREQUENCY: E-mail newsletter/ Daily

DESCRIPTION:
News bulletin.

COVERAGE: Global

RATES:
$50 per ad if via e-mail only; $25 if ad also appears in Email News or Gaea.

RECRUITING SECTION: Advanced Technologies

AUDIENCE CHARACTERISTICS:
- Postgraduate Degree Holders
- Higher Education
- Sciences

ADVERTISING CONTACT:
Dr. Joanne Kluessendorf
Editor
PH: (217) 367-5916
ads@awg.org

AWG Web site

Association for Women Geoscientists
University of Illinois
Dept. of Geology
1301 W. Green St.
Urbana, IL 61801
PH: (217) 367-5916
www.awg.org
ads@awg.org

TYPE/ FREQUENCY: Web site/ Daily

DESCRIPTION:
Association web site.

COVERAGE: Global

RATES:
$50 for full text posting; $30 for a link to your web site URL.

RECRUITING SECTION: Advanced Technologies

AUDIENCE CHARACTERISTICS:
- Postgraduate Degree Holders
- Higher Education
- Sciences

ADVERTISING CONTACT:
Dr. Joanne Kluessendorf
Editor
PH: (217) 367-5916
ads@awg.org

AWIP

Association of Professional Insurance Women
582 New Loudon Rd.
Latham, NY 12110
PH: (518) 785-0721
FAX: (518) 785-3579
www.apiw.org
info@apiw.org

TYPE/ FREQUENCY: Web site/ Daily

DESCRIPTION:
Association dedicated to the advancement of professional insurance women.

COVERAGE: Global

RATES:
Open to members only.

RECRUITING SECTION: Professionals

AUDIENCE CHARACTERISTICS:
- College Graduates
- Insurance

ADVERTISING CONTACT:
Job Bank
PH: (518) 785-0721
FAX: (518) 785-3579
info@apiw.org

AWIS Magazine

Association for Women in Science
1200 New York Ave. NW
#650
Washington, DC 20005
PH: (202) 326-8940
FAX: (202) 326-8960
www.awis.org
awis@awis.org

TYPE/ FREQUENCY: Magazine/ Quarterly

DESCRIPTION:
Association to promote women in science. Over 50% of members have a PhD.

CIRCULATION/ AUDITED BY: 5,000

COVERAGE: USA

RATES:
$300 per month for magazine.

RECRUITING SECTION: Advanced Technologies

AUDIENCE CHARACTERISTICS:
- Postgraduate Degree Holders
- Sciences

ADVERTISING CONTACT:
Kathy Ruby
AWIS Publications Manager
PH: (202) 326-8940
FAX: (202) 326-8960
ruby@awis.org

AWIS.org

Association for Women in Science
1200 New York Ave. NW, #650
Washington, DC 20005
PH: (202) 326-8940
FAX: (202) 326-8960
www.awis.org
awis@awis.org

TYPE/ FREQUENCY: Web site/ Weekly

DESCRIPTION:
Association to promote women in science. Over 50% of members have a PhD.

COVERAGE: Global

RATES:
$100 additional for web site (ads cost $300 for magazine).

RECRUITING SECTION: Advanced Technologies

AUDIENCE CHARACTERISTICS:
• Postgraduate Degree Holders
• Sciences

ADVERTISING CONTACT:
Kathy Ruby
AWIS Publications Manager
PH: (202) 326-8940
FAX: (202) 326-8960
ruby@awis.org

AWM

Association for Women in Mathematics
4114 Computer and Space Sciences Building
University of Maryland
College Park, MD 20742-2461
PH: (301) 405-7892
FAX: (301) 314-9363
www.awm-math.org
awm@math.umd.edu

TYPE/ FREQUENCY: Web site/ Newsletter/ Weekly

DESCRIPTION:
Women mathematicians and statisticians.

CIRCULATION/ AUDITED BY: 10,000

COVERAGE: Global

RATES:
Online classifieds: 25¢ per word per day or $150 for 100 words for 60 days.

RECRUITING SECTION: General Recruitment

AUDIENCE CHARACTERISTICS:
• College Graduates
• Sciences

ADVERTISING CONTACT:
Ads
PH: (301) 405-7892
FAX: (301) 314-9363
awm-ads@awm-math.org

AWMI

Association of Women in the Metal Industries
515 King St., #420
Alexandria, VA 22314-3137
PH: (703) 739-8335
FAX: (703) 684-6048
www.awmi.com
trideout@clarionmr.com

TYPE/ FREQUENCY: Web site/ Daily

DESCRIPTION:
AWMI was founded to foster the professionalism and personal growth of women in the metal industries.

COVERAGE: Global

RATES:
Contact for rates.

RECRUITING SECTION: Professionals

AUDIENCE CHARACTERISTICS:
• Industrial

ADVERTISING CONTACT:
Tonya Rideout
Advertising
PH: (703) 739-8335

AWP

Association of Women Professionals
PO Box 5560
Chicago , IL 60680
PH: (773) 363-5659
www.awoman.bizland.com
awoman@bizland.com

TYPE/ FREQUENCY: Web site/ Daily

DESCRIPTION:
Association supporting the advancement of professional women.

COVERAGE: Global

RATES:
$25 per month per listing.

RECRUITING SECTION: Professionals

AUDIENCE CHARACTERISTICS:
• College Graduates

ADVERTISING CONTACT:
Job Bank
PH: (773) 363-5659
awoman@bizland.com

AWRT CareerLine

American Women in Radio and Television
1595 Spring Hill Rd., #330
Vienna, VA 22182
PH: (703) 506-3290
FAX: (703) 506-3266
www.awrt.org
info@awrt.org

TYPE/ FREQUENCY: Fax-on-demand list/ Biweekly

DESCRIPTION:
AWRT provides a voice for women in the electronic media and its allied fields.

COVERAGE: USA

RATES:
Free.

RECRUITING SECTION: Professionals

AUDIENCE CHARACTERISTICS:
• College Graduates
• Communications

ADVERTISING CONTACT:
Publications
PH: (703) 506-3290
FAX: (703) 506-3266

AWSCPA

American Society of Women CPAs
Administrative Offices
136 S. Keowee St.
Dayton, OH 45402
PH: (800) AWSCPA-1
FAX: (937) 222-5794
www.awscpa.org
info@awscpa.org

TYPE/ FREQUENCY: Web site/ Daily

DESCRIPTION:
An organization for women CPAs.

COVERAGE: Global

RATES:
Insert fee $30; 100 words or less $25; up to 200 words 25¢ per word; additional months per word 15¢. (Insert fee will be waived if AWSCPA headquarters is notified prior to posting removal date.)

RECRUITING SECTION: Professionals

AUDIENCE CHARACTERISTICS:
• Accounting

ADVERTISING CONTACT:
Career Opportunities
PH: (937) 222-1872
FAX: (937) 222-5794
info@awscpa.org

The Baltimore Afro-American

The Afro-American Newspaper Co.
Classifieds
2519 N. Charles St.
Baltimore, MD 21218
PH: (410) 554-8200
FAX: (410) 554-8213

TYPE/ FREQUENCY: Newspaper/ Weekly

DESCRIPTION:
Serving the African American community in Baltimore.

CIRCULATION/ AUDITED BY: 45,000

COVERAGE: Baltimore, MD

RATES:
$22.26 per column inch.

RECRUITING SECTION: General Recruitment

AUDIENCE CHARACTERISTICS:
• College Graduates

ADVERTISING CONTACT:
Bill Smith
Classifieds
PH: (410) 554-8200
FAX: (410) 554-8213

BDPA Job Listings

National Black Data Processing Associates
9315 Largo Dr. W, #260
Largo, MD 20774
PH: (800) 727-BDPA
FAX: (301) 350-0052
www.bdpa.org

TYPE/ FREQUENCY: Web site/ Daily

DESCRIPTION:
Ninety-five percent of BDPA are employed in information technology areas.

COVERAGE: Global

RATES:
$100 per job per 30-day listing.

RECRUITING SECTION: Advanced Technologies

AUDIENCE CHARACTERISTICS:
• College Graduates
• High-Tech
• Computers/Information Technology

ADVERTISING CONTACT:
Advertising
PH: (301) 350-0001
FAX: (301) 350-0052

BDPA Journal Online

National Black Data Processing Associates
9315 Largo Dr. W, #260
Largo, MD 20774
PH: (800) 727-BDPA
FAX: (301) 350-0052
www.bdpa.org

TYPE/ FREQUENCY: Web site/ Quarterly

DESCRIPTION:
Ninety-five percent of BDPA are employed in information technology areas.

COVERAGE: Global

RATES:
$1,000 per quarter.

RECRUITING SECTION: Advanced Technologies

AUDIENCE CHARACTERISTICS:
• College Graduates
• High-Tech
• Computers/Information Technology

ADVERTISING CONTACT:
Advertising
PH: (301) 350-0001
FAX: (301) 350-0052

BIGnet.org

Blacks in Government
1820 11th St. NW
Washington, DC 20001
PH: (202) 667-3280
FAX: (202) 667-3705
www.bignet.org

TYPE/ FREQUENCY: Web site/ Weekly

DESCRIPTION:
Organization supporting Blacks in public service.

COVERAGE: Global

RATES:
Free.

RECRUITING SECTION: Professionals

AUDIENCE CHARACTERISTICS:
• Government

ADVERTISING CONTACT:
Opportunities
PH: (202) 667-3280
FAX: (202) 667-3705

The Black Chronicle

PO Box 17498
Oklahoma City, OK 73136
PH: (405) 424-4695
FAX: (405) 424-6708

TYPE/ FREQUENCY: Newspaper/ Weekly

DESCRIPTION:
African American community news.

CIRCULATION/ AUDITED BY: 30,088/ CPVS

COVERAGE: Oklahoma City, OK

RATES:
$16.44 per column inch.

RECRUITING SECTION: General Recruitment

AUDIENCE CHARACTERISTICS:
• High School Graduates, College Graduates

ADVERTISING CONTACT:
Tiffany Cooper
Advertising
PH: (405) 424-9525
FAX: (405) 424-6708

The Black Collegian

iMinorities, Inc.
909 Poydras St.
36th Floor
New Orleans, LA 70112
PH: (504) 523-0154
FAX: (504) 598-3894
www.black-collegian.com

TYPE/ FREQUENCY: Magazine/ Biannually

DESCRIPTION:
The career and self-development magazine for African American students; published twice a year.

COVERAGE: USA

RATES:
Job opportunities listing: $1,050 one issue; repeat rate $950; double issue rate $2,000.

RECRUITING SECTION: General Recruitment

AUDIENCE CHARACTERISTICS:
• College Students/Recent Graduates

ADVERTISING CONTACT:
Pres Edwards
Black Collegian Magazine
PH: (504) 523-0514
FAX: (504) 598-3894

Black Engineer and Information Technology

Career Communications Group, Inc.
729 E. Pratt St., #504
Baltimore, MD 21202
PH: (410) 244-7107
FAX: (410) 752-1834
www.ccgmag.com

TYPE/ FREQUENCY: Magazine/ Quarterly

DESCRIPTION:
Targeted to African American professionals and students in science and technology.

CIRCULATION/ AUDITED BY: 15,000

COVERAGE: USA

RATES:
1/2 page b/w $3,195.

RECRUITING SECTION: Advanced Technologies

AUDIENCE CHARACTERISTICS:
• College Graduates
• High-Tech
• Sciences, Engineering

ADVERTISING CONTACT:
Advertising
PH: (410) 244-7107
FAX: (410) 752-1834

Black Enterprise Magazine

Earl Graves Publishing Co. Inc.
130 5th Ave.
New York, NY 10011-4399
PH: (212) 242-8000
FAX: (212) 886-9618
www.blackenterprise.com
benyc_ads@blackenterprise.com

TYPE/ FREQUENCY: Magazine/ Monthly

DESCRIPTION:
A magazine targeted to black professionals, managers, corporate executives, and entrepreneurs.

CIRCULATION/ AUDITED BY: 475,000/ ABC

COVERAGE: USA

RATES:
1/6 page $7,890; 1/2 page $17,095 single run b/w.

RECRUITING SECTION: Managers and Executives

AUDIENCE CHARACTERISTICS:
• College Graduates

ADVERTISING CONTACT:
Kathy Alvia
Advertising
PH: (212) 886-9618
FAX: (212) 886-9548
alviak@blackenterprise.com

Black Issues in Higher Education

Black Issues in Higher Education
10520 Warwick Ave., #B-8
Fairfax , VA 22030
PH: (703) 385-2981
FAX: (703) 385-1839
www.blackissues.com
biads@cmabiccw.com

TYPE/ FREQUENCY: Magazine/ Biweekly

DESCRIPTION:
Readership includes administrators, faculty, business officers, student service professionals, librarians, technology directors, and historically Black colleges and universities.

CIRCULATION/ AUDITED BY: 40,000

COVERAGE: USA

RATES:
1/2 page b/w $1,235; 1/6 page b/w $550.

RECRUITING SECTION: Professionals

AUDIENCE CHARACTERISTICS:
• College Graduates
• Higher Education

ADVERTISING CONTACT:
Advertising
PH: (703) 385-2981
FAX: (703) 385-1839
biads@cmabiccw.com

Black MBA Magazine

iMinorities, Inc.
909 Poydras St., 36th Floor
New Orleans, LA 70112
PH: (504) 523-0154
FAX: (504) 598-3894
www.iminorities.com
michelle@imdiversity.com

TYPE/ FREQUENCY: Magazine/ Biannually

DESCRIPTION:
Official publication for the National Black MBA Association; two issues: conference issue in September, career issue in January.

CIRCULATION/ AUDITED BY: 29,275/ BPA

COVERAGE: USA

RATES:
Full page b/w $6,100 per issue, $11,500 both issues; 1/2 page b/w $4,100 per issue, $7,500 both issues.

RECRUITING SECTION: Professionals

AUDIENCE CHARACTERISTICS:
• Postgraduate Degree Holders

ADVERTISING CONTACT:
Michelle Ancar
Black MBA Magazine
PH: (504) 523-0154 ext. 301
FAX: (504) 598-3894
michelle@iminorities.com

Black MBA Magazine

National Black MBA Association
180 N. Michigan Ave., #1400
Chicago, IL 60601
PH: (312) 236-2622
FAX: (312) 236-4131
www.nbmbaa.org
mail@nbmbaa.org

TYPE/ FREQUENCY: Magazine/ Quarterly

DESCRIPTION:
Official magazine of the National Black MBA Association.

COVERAGE: USA

RATES:
Contact for rates.

RECRUITING SECTION: Managers and Executives

AUDIENCE CHARACTERISTICS:
• Postgraduate Degree Holders

ADVERTISING CONTACT:
Black MBA Magazine
PH: (312) 236-2622
FAX: (312) 236-4131
mail@nbmbaa.org

Black News

South Carolina Media Group
1310 Harden St.
Columbia, SC 29204
PH: (803) 799-5252
FAX: (803) 799-7709
www.scblackmedia.com
scbnews@aol.com

TYPE/ FREQUENCY: Newspaper/ Weekly

DESCRIPTION:
African American community news.

CIRCULATION/ AUDITED BY: 76,978

COVERAGE: SC

RATES:
Classifieds: $22.50 per column inch.

RECRUITING SECTION: General Recruitment

AUDIENCE CHARACTERISTICS:
• College Graduates, High School Graduates, Trade/Professional School Graduates

ADVERTISING CONTACT:
Ruth Carlton
Sales Representative
PH: (803) 799-5252
FAX: (803) 799-7709
scbnews@aol.com

The Black Perspective

E. M. Publishing Enterprises
19456 Ventura Blvd., #200
Tarzana, CA 91356
PH: (818) 774-0870
FAX: (818) 654-0874
empei@aol.com

TYPE/ FREQUENCY: Magazine/ Quarterly

DESCRIPTION:
Publication is dedicated to the interests and concerns of our Black community.

CIRCULATION/ AUDITED BY: 7,500/ BPA

COVERAGE: USA

RATES:
Contact for rates.

RECRUITING SECTION: Professionals

AUDIENCE CHARACTERISTICS:
• College Graduates

ADVERTISING CONTACT:
Dariush Pasha
Sales Manager
PH: (818) 774-1931
FAX: (818) 654-0874

BlackEnterprise.com

Black Enterprise Career Channel
130 5th Ave.
New York, NY 10011
PH: (212) 242-0280
FAX: (212) 886-9618
www.blackenterprise.com

TYPE/ FREQUENCY: Web site/ Daily

DESCRIPTION:
"Premier" site on the Internet for African American entrepreneurs. Career pages powered by CareerBuilder.com.

COVERAGE: Global

RATES:
$175 per job; packages available.

RECRUITING SECTION: Professionals

ADVERTISING CONTACT:
CareerBuilder.com
PH: (888) 670-8326

BlackStocks.com

Strategic Interactive Media, Inc.
South Park Towers, 12th Floor
6000 Fairview Rd.
Charlotte, NC 28210
PH: (704) 596-3553
FAX: (704) 234-6088
www.blackstocks.com
info@blackstocks.com

TYPE/ FREQUENCY: Web site/ Daily

DESCRIPTION:
An African American investment and online trading site. Career Center is powered by HeadHunter.net

COVERAGE: Global

RATES:
$100 per job per month; packages available.

RECRUITING SECTION: Professionals

AUDIENCE CHARACTERISTICS:
• College Graduates
• Investment

ADVERTISING CONTACT:
HeadHunter.net
PH: (877) 235-8978

BlackVoices Career Fairs

BlackVoices.com
Tribune Towers
435 N. Michigan Ave., #LL2
Chicago, IL 60611
PH: (312) 222-4326
FAX: (312) 222-4502
www.blackvoices.com

TYPE/ FREQUENCY: Career fair/ Quarterly

DESCRIPTION:
With more than 600,000 registered members, Black Voices is "the premier web site for African-Americans." They cosponsor career fairs with local partners.

COVERAGE: USA

RATES:
Contact for rates.

RECRUITING SECTION: Professionals

AUDIENCE CHARACTERISTICS:
• College Graduates

ADVERTISING CONTACT:
PH: (312) 222-3739

BlackVoices.com

Tribune Towers
435 N. Michigan Ave., #LL2
Chicago, IL 60611
PH: (312) 222-4326
FAX: (312) 222-4502
www.blackvoices.com

TYPE/ FREQUENCY: Web site/ Daily

DESCRIPTION:
With more than 600,000 registered members, Black Voices is "the premier web site for African-Americans." The career center is powered by CareerBuilder.com.

CIRCULATION/ AUDITED BY: 600,000

COVERAGE: Global

RATES:
$175 per job.

RECRUITING SECTION: Professionals

AUDIENCE CHARACTERISTICS:
• College Graduates

ADVERTISING CONTACT:
CareerBuilder.com
PH: (888) 670-8326

Blackworld.com

Blackworld
41 Sutter St., #1319
San Francisco, CA 94104
PH: (510) 405-2047
FAX: (510) 405-2047
www.blackworld.com

TYPE/ FREQUENCY: Web site/ Daily

DESCRIPTION:
An Internet site devoted to the African American community. Career Center is powered by HeadHunter.net.

COVERAGE: Global

RATES:
$100 per job per month; packages available.

RECRUITING SECTION: General Recruitment

AUDIENCE CHARACTERISTICS:
• College Graduates

ADVERTISING CONTACT:
HeadHunter.net
PH: (877) 235-8978

BlueSuitMom.com

BlueSuitMom.com, Inc.
110 E. Broward Blvd., #1400
Fort Lauderdale, FL 33301
PH: (954) 468-4752
FAX: (954) 468-4791
www.bluesuitmom.com

TYPE/ FREQUENCY: Web site/ Daily

DESCRIPTION:
Organization supporting working mothers. Career center powered by HeadHunter.net.

COVERAGE: Global

RATES:
$100 per job per month; packages available.

RECRUITING SECTION: General Recruitment

AUDIENCE CHARACTERISTICS:
• College Graduates

ADVERTISING CONTACT:
HeadHunter.net
PH: (877) 235-8978

Boston Chapter of NAAAP

National Association of Asian American Professionals
PO Box 381435
Cambridge, MA 02238-1435
PH: (781) 937-7072
www.naaapboston.org

TYPE/ FREQUENCY: Web site/ Monthly

DESCRIPTION:
Asian professional organization with chapters around the country.

COVERAGE: Global

RATES:
Sponsorship opportunities available for convention and professional development.

RECRUITING SECTION: Professionals

AUDIENCE CHARACTERISTICS:
• College Graduates

ADVERTISING CONTACT:
Corporate Sponsorship
PH: (781) 937-7072
naaap@naaapboston.org

The Bottom Line

National Society of Hispanic MBAs
8204 Elmbrook, #235
Dallas, TX 75247
PH: (877) 467-4622
FAX: (214) 267-1626
www.nshmba.org
info@nshmba.org

TYPE/ FREQUENCY: Newsletter/ Monthly

DESCRIPTION:
Monthly publication of the society.

CIRCULATION/ AUDITED BY: 5,000

COVERAGE: USA

RATES:
1/4 page b/w $750 per insertion; full page b/w $1,500 per insertion.

RECRUITING SECTION: Managers and Executives

AUDIENCE CHARACTERISTICS:
• Postgraduate Degree Holders
• Spanish Language

ADVERTISING CONTACT:
Jim Greene
Greene Marketing Services
PH: (214) 526-1840
gmsvc@aol.com

The Brasilian

The Brasilian Press
PO Box 985
New York, NY 10185
PH: (212) 382-1630
FAX: (212) 382-1632
thebrasiliantimes@aol.com

TYPE/ FREQUENCY: Newspaper/ Monthly

DESCRIPTION:
The oldest bilingual Portuguese newspaper in the United States.

CIRCULATION/ AUDITED BY: 45,000

COVERAGE: USA

RATES:
$25 per issue.

RECRUITING SECTION: General Recruitment

AUDIENCE CHARACTERISTICS:
• Portuguese Language

ADVERTISING CONTACT:
Classifieds
PH: (212) 398-6464
FAX: (212) 382-3620
thebrasiliantimes@aol.com

Business-Disability.com

National Business and Disability Council
201 I U Willets Rd.
Albertson, NY 11507
PH: (516) 465-1520
www.business-disability.com
info@business-disability.com

TYPE/ FREQUENCY: Web site/ Daily

DESCRIPTION:
The leading national corporate resource for the successful integration of persons with disabilities into the workforce and consumer marketplace.

COVERAGE: Global

RATES:
Must be a member to post jobs (free service); membership levels: Gold $5,000 annually; Silver $2,500 annually.

RECRUITING SECTION: General Recruitment

AUDIENCE CHARACTERISTICS:
• High School Graduates, College Graduates

ADVERTISING CONTACT:
Marketing
PH: (516) 465-1520
kilarjian@business-disability.com

BVQ Magazine

BlackVoices.com
Tribune Towers
435 N. Michigan Ave., #LL2
Chicago, IL 60611
PH: (312) 222-4326
FAX: (312) 222-4502
www.blackvoices.com

TYPE/ FREQUENCY: Magazine/ Quarterly

DESCRIPTION:
With more than 600,000 registered members, Black Voices is "the premier web site for African-Americans." This is their official magazine.

CIRCULATION/ AUDITED BY: 7,500/ BPA

COVERAGE: USA

RATES:
Contact for rates.

RECRUITING SECTION: Professionals

AUDIENCE CHARACTERISTICS:
• College Graduates

ADVERTISING CONTACT:
Bretland Moore
PH: (212) 527-8796
bmoore@corp.blackvoices.com

The California Advocate

1715 E St., #108
Fresno, CA 93706
PH: (559) 268-0941
FAX: (559) 268-0943
www.caladvocate.com
info@caladvocate.com

TYPE/ FREQUENCY: Newspaper

DESCRIPTION:
African American community paper serving Fresno area. Less than 15% of Advocate readers claim a subscription to any other newspaper.

CIRCULATION/ AUDITED BY: 156,039

COVERAGE: Fresno, CA

RATES:
$39.50 per column inch.

RECRUITING SECTION: General Recruitment

AUDIENCE CHARACTERISTICS:
• High School Graduates, College Graduates

ADVERTISING CONTACT:
Advertising
PH: (559) 268-0941
FAX: (559) 268-0943
info@caladvocate.com

The Capitol Times

814 San Jacinto, #203
Austin, TX 78701
PH: (512) 499-8660
FAX: (512) 499-8228
www.capitoltimes.com
swalker@austin.rr.com

TYPE/ FREQUENCY: Newspaper/ Weekly

DESCRIPTION:
African American community newspaper.

COVERAGE: Austin, TX

RATES:
Classified rate: $21.50 per column inch.

RECRUITING SECTION: General Recruitment

AUDIENCE CHARACTERISTICS:
• College Graduates

ADVERTISING CONTACT:
Sedric Walker
Classifieds
PH: (512) 499-8660
FAX: (512) 488-8228
swalker@austin.rr.com

Career Opportunity and Exchange

National Association of Hispanic Journalists
1193 National Press Building
Washington, DC 20045-2100
PH: (888) 346-NAHJ
FAX: (202) 662-7144
www.nahj.org
nahj@nahj.org

TYPE/ FREQUENCY: Web site/ Weekly

DESCRIPTION:
Hispanic professional journalists.

COVERAGE: Global

RATES:
Free.

RECRUITING SECTION: Professionals

AUDIENCE CHARACTERISTICS:
- College Graduates
- Communications
- Spanish Language

ADVERTISING CONTACT:
Career Resources
PH: (888) 346-NAHJ
FAX: (202) 662-7144
nahj@nahj.org

Careers and the Disabled

Equal Opportunity Publications, Inc.
445 Broad Hollow Rd., #425
Melville, NY 11747
PH: (631) 421-9421
FAX: (631) 421-0359
www.eop.com
info@eop.com

TYPE/ FREQUENCY: Magazine/ Five times per year

DESCRIPTION:
The nation's first and only career guidance/recruitment magazine for persons with disabilities who are at college, graduate, or professional levels.

CIRCULATION/ AUDITED BY: 10,500

COVERAGE: USA

RATES:
$250 per month per magazine for online editions; call for print rates.

RECRUITING SECTION: General Recruitment

AUDIENCE CHARACTERISTICS:
- College Graduates

ADVERTISING CONTACT:
Advertising
PH: (631) 421-9421
FAX: (631) 421-0359
info@eop.com

Careers and the Disabled Career Fair

Equal Opportunity Publications, Inc.
445 Broad Hollow Rd., #425
Melville, NY 11747
PH: (631) 421-9421
FAX: (631) 421-0359
www.eop.com
info@eop.com

TYPE/ FREQUENCY: Career fair/ Biannually

DESCRIPTION:
Career fair promoting job opportunities for persons with disabilities.

COVERAGE: USA

RATES:
Contact for rates.

RECRUITING SECTION: General Recruitment

AUDIENCE CHARACTERISTICS:
- College Graduates

ADVERTISING CONTACT:
Advertising
PH: (631) 421-9421
FAX: (631) 421-0359
info@eop.com

Careers On-Line

Disability Services, University of Minnesota
University of Minnesota
University Gateway, #180
200 Oak St. SE
Minneapolis, MN 55455
PH: (612) 626-9649
www.disserv.stu.umn.edu
careers@disserv.stu.umn.edu

TYPE/ FREQUENCY: Web site/ Daily

DESCRIPTION:
Careers On-Line is a federally funded project that provides job search and employment information through accessible technology to persons with disabilities.

COVERAGE: Global

RATES:
Free.

RECRUITING SECTION: General Recruitment

AUDIENCE CHARACTERISTICS:
- College Students, Recent Graduates

ADVERTISING CONTACT:
Disabilities Services
PH: (612) 626-9649

Careerwoman2000.com

Diversity Village Inc.
287 E. 6th St., #200
St. Paul, MN 55105
PH: (651) 224-0330
FAX: (651) 224-0740
www.careerwoman2000.com

TYPE/ FREQUENCY: Web site/ Daily

DESCRIPTION:
Web site providing recruitment and career resources to women.

COVERAGE: Global

RATES:
Contact for rates.

RECRUITING SECTION: Professionals

AUDIENCE CHARACTERISTICS:
• College Graduates

ADVERTISING CONTACT:
Omar Salas
Sales
PH: (651) 224-0330
FAX: (651) 224-0740

CareerWomen.com

Career Exposure
1881 S.W. Front Ave.
Portland, OR 97201
PH: (503) 525-8498
www.careerwomen.com
bizmail@careerwomen.com

TYPE/ FREQUENCY: Web site/ Daily

DESCRIPTION:
A women-owned business helping women achieve success in their careers and lives.

COVERAGE: Global

RATES:
$89 per job posting per month.

RECRUITING SECTION: Professionals

AUDIENCE CHARACTERISTICS:
• College Graduates

ADVERTISING CONTACT:
Job Posting
PH: (503) 525-8498
bizmail@careerwomen.com

Carib News

New York Carib News
28 W. 39th St.
New York, NY 10018
PH: (914) 944-1991
FAX: (212) 944-2089
nycarib@aol.com

TYPE/ FREQUENCY: Newspaper/ Weekly

DESCRIPTION:
Caribbean community newspaper.

CIRCULATION/ AUDITED BY: 67,000

COVERAGE: New York, NY

RATES:
Classifieds: $31.55 for 25-30 words; $1 each additional word.

RECRUITING SECTION: General Recruitment

AUDIENCE CHARACTERISTICS:
• High School Graduates, College Graduates

ADVERTISING CONTACT:
Classifieds
PH: (212) 944-1991
FAX: (212) 944-2089
nycarib@aol.com

CASPA

Chinese American Semiconductor Professional Association
3515 Ryder St.
Santa Clara, CA 95051
PH: (408) 245-5638
FAX: (408) 245-5638
www.caspa.com
caspa@ix.netcom.com

TYPE/ FREQUENCY: Web site/ Monthly

DESCRIPTION:
Semiconductor industry association.

CIRCULATION/ AUDITED BY: 1,000

COVERAGE: Global

RATES:
Contact for rates.

RECRUITING SECTION: Advanced Technologies

AUDIENCE CHARACTERISTICS:
• College Graduates
• High-Tech
• Computers/Information Technology, Sciences, Engineering
• Chinese Language

ADVERTISING CONTACT:
Corporate Memberships
PH: (408) 245-5638
FAX: (408) 245-5638
caspa@ix.netcom.com

CCNMA

California Chicano News Media Association
3800 S. Figueroa St.
Los Angeles, CA 90037-1206
PH: (213) 743-4960
FAX: (213) 743-4989
www.ccnma.org
info@ccnma.org

TYPE/ FREQUENCY: Web site/ Daily

DESCRIPTION:
An organization for journalists, media professionals, employers, and students.

COVERAGE: Global

RATES:
Free job postings.

RECRUITING SECTION: Professionals

AUDIENCE CHARACTERISTICS:
• Communications
• Spanish Language

ADVERTISING CONTACT:
Job Openings
PH: (213) 743-4960
FAX: (213) 743-4989
info@ccnma.org

Center on Employment

National Technology Institute for the Deaf
Rochester Institute for Technology
Rochester, NY 14623
PH: (716) 475-6834
www.ntidweb.rit.edu

TYPE/ FREQUENCY: Web site/ Daily

DESCRIPTION:
The world's first and largest technical college for the deaf and hard of hearing. Career center offers job postings and campus interview visits.

COVERAGE: Global

RATES:
Free.

RECRUITING SECTION: Advanced Technologies

AUDIENCE CHARACTERISTICS:
• College Students/Recent Graduates

ADVERTISING CONTACT:
Career Center
PH: (716) 475-6834

Center on Employment

National Technology Institute for the Deaf
Rochester Institute for Technology
Rochester, NY 14623
PH: (716) 475-6834
www.ntidweb.rit.edu

TYPE/ FREQUENCY: Career fair/ Annually

DESCRIPTION:
The world's first and largest technical college for the deaf and hard of hearing. 2001 marked NTIDs first career fair for the deaf.

COVERAGE: Rochester, NY

RATES:
Contact for rates.

RECRUITING SECTION: Advanced Technologies

AUDIENCE CHARACTERISTICS:
• College Students/Recent Graduates

ADVERTISING CONTACT:
Career Center
PH: (716) 475-6834

Challenger Newspaper

Challenger News Network
PO Drawer 1679
Wilmington, NC 28402
PH: (800) 462-0738
FAX: (910) 763-6304
www.challengernews.com

TYPE/ FREQUENCY: Newspaper/ Weekly

DESCRIPTION:
Serves as the official home of the National Black Family Empowerment Agenda Network representing the business and community interests of millions of African Americans.

CIRCULATION/ AUDITED BY: 5,000

COVERAGE: USA

RATES:
$2.50 per line.

RECRUITING SECTION: General Recruitment

AUDIENCE CHARACTERISTICS:
• College Graduates

ADVERTISING CONTACT:
Kathy Grear
Personnel and Display Sales
PH: (800) 462-0738
FAX: (910) 763-6304
kgrear@challengernews.com

Charlotte Post

1531 Camden Rd.
Charlotte, NC 28203
PH: (704) 376-0496
FAX: (704) 342-2160
www.thecharlottepost.com

TYPE/ FREQUENCY: Newspaper/ Weekly

DESCRIPTION:
African American community news.

CIRCULATION/ AUDITED BY: 23,278

COVERAGE: Charlotte, NC

RATES:
Display classified: $11.37 net per column inch; regular verbiage: 70¢ per word with a $12 minimum.

RECRUITING SECTION: General Recruitment

AUDIENCE CHARACTERISTICS:
• High School Graduates, College Graduates

ADVERTISING CONTACT:
Classifieds
PH: (704) 376-0496
FAX: (704) 342-2160

Cherokee Phoenix

Cherokee Phoenix and Indian Advocate
PO Box 948
Tahlequah, OK 74465-0948
PH: (918) 456-0671
FAX: (918) 458-6136

TYPE/ FREQUENCY: Newspaper/ Quarterly

DESCRIPTION:
Native American publication.

CIRCULATION/ AUDITED BY: 96,000

COVERAGE: OK

RATES:
$20 per column inch.

RECRUITING SECTION: General Recruitment

AUDIENCE CHARACTERISTICS:
• High School Graduates, College Graduates

ADVERTISING CONTACT:
Larry Daugherty
Advertising Manager
PH: (918) 456-0671 ext. 2324
FAX: (918) 458-6136
ldaugherty@cherokee.org

The Chicago Shimpo

The Chicago Shimpo/Japanese American News
4670 N. Manor Ave.
Chicago, IL 60625
PH: (773) 478-6170
FAX: (773) 478-9360
shimpo@mc.net

TYPE/ FREQUENCY: Newspaper/ Biweekly

DESCRIPTION:
Serving the bilingual Japanese American community of Chicago.

CIRCULATION/ AUDITED BY: 5,000

COVERAGE: Chicago, IL

RATES:
$12 per line.

RECRUITING SECTION: General Recruitment

AUDIENCE CHARACTERISTICS:
• College Graduates
• Japanese Language

Chicago Standard

Standard Newspapers
615 S. Halsted
Chicago Heights, IL 60411
PH: (312) 755-5021
www.standardnewspapers.com

TYPE/ FREQUENCY: Newspaper/ Weekly

DESCRIPTION:
African American community news.

CIRCULATION/ AUDITED BY: 15,000

COVERAGE: Chicago, IL

RATES:
Contact for rates.

RECRUITING SECTION: General Recruitment

AUDIENCE CHARACTERISTICS:
• High School Graduates, College Graduates

ADVERTISING CONTACT:
PH: (312) 755-5021

Chickasaw Times

Chickasaw Nation
Box 1548
Ada, OK 74821
PH: (580) 332-2977
FAX: (580) 332-3949
times.chickasaw.net
ctimes@wilnet1.com

TYPE/ FREQUENCY: Newspaper/ Monthly

DESCRIPTION:
Official newspaper of the Chickasaw Nation.

CIRCULATION/ AUDITED BY: 17,000

COVERAGE: OK

RATES:
$5 per column inch.

RECRUITING SECTION: General Recruitment

AUDIENCE CHARACTERISTICS:
• High School Graduates, College Graduates, Trade/Professional
  School Graduates

ADVERTISING CONTACT:
PH: (580) 332-2977
FAX: (580) 332-3949
ctimes@wilnet1.com

Chinese Software Professionals Assoc. Annual Conference

Chinese Software Professionals Association
PO Box 700249
San Jose, CA 95170-0249
www.cspa.com
cspa@aimnet.com

TYPE/ FREQUENCY: Conference/ Annually

DESCRIPTION:
CSPA serves the interests of Chinese American professionals in Silicon Valley. Annual conference.

CIRCULATION/ AUDITED BY: 2,000

COVERAGE: San Jose, CA

RATES:
Contact for rates.

RECRUITING SECTION: Advanced Technologies

AUDIENCE CHARACTERISTICS:
• College Graduates
• High-Tech
• Computers/Information Technology, Technology
• Chinese Language

ADVERTISING CONTACT:
Conferences
cspa@aimnet.com

Chinese Software Professionals Assoc. Job Fair

Chinese Software Professionals Association
PO Box 700249
San Jose, CA 95170-0249
www.cspa.com
cspa@aimnet.com

TYPE/ FREQUENCY: Career fair/ Annually

DESCRIPTION:
CSPA serves the interests of Chinese American professionals in Silicon Valley. Holds annual career fair.

CIRCULATION/ AUDITED BY: 2,000

COVERAGE: San Jose, CA

RATES:
Contact for rates.

RECRUITING SECTION: Advanced Technologies

AUDIENCE CHARACTERISTICS:
• College Graduates
• High-Tech
• Computers/Information Technology, Technology
• Chinese Language

ADVERTISING CONTACT:
Job Fair
cspa@aimnet.com

The Circle News

The Circle
3355 36th Ave. S
Minneapolis, MN 55406
PH: (612) 722-3686
FAX: (612) 722-3773
www.thecirclenews.org
info@circlenews.org

TYPE/ FREQUENCY: Newspaper/ Monthly

DESCRIPTION:
Native American newspaper.

CIRCULATION/ AUDITED BY: 20,000

COVERAGE: USA

RATES:
Classifieds: $3 per line.

RECRUITING SECTION: General Recruitment

AUDIENCE CHARACTERISTICS:
• High School Graduates, College Graduates

ADVERTISING CONTACT:
Simone Rendon
Advertising Sales Manager
PH: (612) 722-3686
FAX: (612) 722-3773
adsales@thecirclenews.com

Cnetwork

PO Box 391172
Mountainview, CA 94049
PH: (408) 364-1342
FAX: (408) 980-0066
www.cnetwork.org
contact@cnetwork.org

TYPE/ FREQUENCY: Web site/ Daily

DESCRIPTION:
A nonprofit nonpolitical organization dedicated to serving the overseas Chinese community.

CIRCULATION/ AUDITED BY: 2,500

COVERAGE: Global

RATES:
Free, but must be member to post.

RECRUITING SECTION: General Recruitment

AUDIENCE CHARACTERISTICS:
• College Graduates
• Chinese Language

ADVERTISING CONTACT:
Membership
PH: (408) 980-0885
FAX: (408) 980-0066
contact@cnetwork.org

Colton Courier

Inland Empire Community Newspapers
PO Box 6247
San Bernardino, CA 92412
PH: (909) 381-9898
FAX: (909) 384-0406

TYPE/ FREQUENCY: Newspaper/ Weekly

DESCRIPTION:
Community newspaper that reaches a largely Hispanic audience.

CIRCULATION/ AUDITED BY: 98,000

COVERAGE: San Bernadino, CA

RATES:
$16.90 per column inch.

RECRUITING SECTION: General Recruitment

AUDIENCE CHARACTERISTICS:
• Spanish Language

ADVERTISING CONTACT:
Kathy Boswell
Classifieds
PH: (909) 381-9898
FAX: (909) 384-0406

The Columbus Times

The Columbus Times Newspaper
2230 Buena Vista Rd.
Columbus, GA 31907
PH: (706) 324-2404
www.columbustimes.com

TYPE/ FREQUENCY: Newspaper/ Weekly

DESCRIPTION:
African American community news.

CIRCULATION/ AUDITED BY: 20,000

COVERAGE: Columbus, GA

RATES:
1x2 classified on web site $30.

RECRUITING SECTION: General Recruitment

ADVERTISING CONTACT:
Classifieds and Advertising
PH: (706) 324-2404

Committee on Women in Engineering

IEEE - Institute of Electrical and Electronics Engineers
445 Hoes Ln.
PO Box 1331
Piscataway, NJ 08855-1331
PH: (732) 981-0060
FAX: (732) 981-1721
www.ieee.org
customer-service@ieee.org

TYPE/ FREQUENCY: E-mail list/ Monthly

DESCRIPTION:
Professional computer organization's special women's committee.

COVERAGE: Global

RATES:
Free.

RECRUITING SECTION: Advanced Technologies

AUDIENCE CHARACTERISTICS:
• College Graduates
• High-Tech
• Computers/Information Technology, Technology

ADVERTISING CONTACT:
Committee on Women in Engineering
PH: (732) 981-0060
FAX: (732) 981-1721
women@ieee.org

Contempora Magazine

1501 Jefferson St.
Nashville, TN 37208
PH: (615) 321-9551
FAX: (615) 321-0409

TYPE/ FREQUENCY: Magazine/ Bimonthly

DESCRIPTION:
Magazine targeted to affluent African American professionals, managers, and entrepreneurs.

CIRCULATION/ AUDITED BY: 36,000

COVERAGE: Nashville, TN

RATES:
Business card size: $200; 1/2 page $1,185.

RECRUITING SECTION: Professionals

AUDIENCE CHARACTERISTICS:
• College Graduates

ADVERTISING CONTACT:
Bill Thompson
Advertising
PH: (615) 321-9551
FAX: (615) 321-0409

Corporate Gray Online

Competitive Edge Services, Inc.
PO Box 342
Fairfax Station, VA 22039
PH: (703) 690-6381
FAX: (703) 690-1687
www.greentogray.com
susan@corporate-gray.com

TYPE/ FREQUENCY: Web site/ Job fair/ Daily

DESCRIPTION:
Jobs for transitioning servicemembers and veterans.

COVERAGE: Global

RATES:
Job postings are free; unlimited resume searches: 1 month $250;
3 months $600; 6 months $1,100; 1 year $2,000.

RECRUITING SECTION: General Recruitment

AUDIENCE CHARACTERISTICS:
• High School Graduates, College Graduates

ADVERTISING CONTACT:
Sales
PH: (703) 690-6381
FAX: (703) 690-1687
susan@corporate-gray.com

The Crisis Magazine

NAACP - National Association for the Advancement of Colored
People
4805 Mt. Hope Dr.
Baltimore, MD 21215
PH: (410) 486-9216
FAX: (410) 318-6712
www.thecrisismagazine.com
iartis@naacpnet.org

TYPE/ FREQUENCY: Magazine/ Bimonthly

DESCRIPTION:
The official publication of the NAACP.

CIRCULATION/ AUDITED BY: 250,000/ Simmons Custom
Media Study

COVERAGE: USA

RATES:
Classified rate: $315 per column inch.

RECRUITING SECTION: Professionals

AUDIENCE CHARACTERISTICS:
• College Graduates

ADVERTISING CONTACT:
India Artis
PH: (410) 486-9216
FAX: (410) 318-6712
iartis@naacpnet.org

CSPA Newsletter

Chinese Software Professionals Association
PO Box 700249
San Jose, CA 95170-0249
www.cspa.com
cspa@aimnet.com

TYPE/ FREQUENCY: Newsletter/ Quarterly

DESCRIPTION:
CSPA serves the interests of Chinese American professionals in
Silicon Valley. Newsletter has job postings.

CIRCULATION/ AUDITED BY: 2,000

COVERAGE: San Jose, CA

RATES:
Contact for rates.

RECRUITING SECTION: Advanced Technologies

AUDIENCE CHARACTERISTICS:
• College Graduates
• High-Tech
• Advanced Technologies, Computers/Information Technology,
  Technology
• Chinese Language

ADVERTISING CONTACT:
Newsletter
cspa@aimnet.com

CSPA.com

Chinese Software Professionals Association
PO Box 700249
San Jose, CA 95170-0249
www.cspa.com
cspa@aimnet.com

TYPE/ FREQUENCY: Web site/ Daily

DESCRIPTION:
CSPA serves the interests of Chinese American professionals in
Silicon Valley. Web site has job postings.

CIRCULATION/ AUDITED BY: 2,000

COVERAGE: CA

RATES:
Contact for rates.

RECRUITING SECTION: Advanced Technologies

AUDIENCE CHARACTERISTICS:
• College Graduates
• High-Tech
• Computers/Information Technology, Technology
• Chinese Language

ADVERTISING CONTACT:
Job Postings
cspa@aimnet.com

Daily Post Tribune

PO Box 763939
Dallas, TX 75376-3939
PH: (214) 946-7678
FAX: (214) 946-6823
www.dallaspost.com

TYPE/ FREQUENCY: Newspaper/ Weekly

DESCRIPTION:
African American community newspaper.

CIRCULATION/ AUDITED BY: 18,500/ CPVS

COVERAGE: Dallas, TX

RATES:
Local classified rate: $20 per column inch; national rate: $35 per column inch.

RECRUITING SECTION: General Recruitment

AUDIENCE CHARACTERISTICS:
• College Graduates

ADVERTISING CONTACT:
Advertising
PH: (214) 946-7678
FAX: (214) 946-6823

Denver Indian Center Job Board

Denver Indian Center
4407 Morrison Rd.
Denver, CO 80219
PH: (303) 936-2688
FAX: (303) 936-2699
www.denverindiancenter.org
anselma@denverindiancenter.org

TYPE/ FREQUENCY: Resource center/ Web site/ Daily

DESCRIPTION:
The Denver Indian Center, Inc., serves a diverse group of tribes.

CIRCULATION/ AUDITED BY: 18,000

COVERAGE: Denver, CO

RATES:
Free.

RECRUITING SECTION: General Recruitment

AUDIENCE CHARACTERISTICS:
• High School Graduates, College Graduates

ADVERTISING CONTACT:
Anselma Mitchell
Workforce Development
PH: (303) 936-2688
FAX: (303) 936-2699
anselma@denverindiancenter.org

Destinygrp.com

The Destiny Group
750 B St., #1840
San Diego, CA 92101
PH: (619) 696-8700
FAX: (619) 696-8795
www.destinygrp.com
info@destinygrp.com

TYPE/ FREQUENCY: Web site/ Daily

DESCRIPTION:
Connects corporations with the military community.

COVERAGE: Global

RATES:
$150 per job per month; $1,000 per 5 changing jobs per year; $3,000 unlimited job posting per year.

RECRUITING SECTION: General Recruitment

ADVERTISING CONTACT:
Christina
PH: (619) 696-8700
FAX: (619) 696-8795
info@destinygrp.com

DiversiLink

Innovative Human Resources Solutions
PMB 360
801 W. El Camino Real
Mountain View, CA 94040-2511
PH: (650) 962-0235
FAX: (408) 273-6467
www.diversilink.com
sales@diversilink.com

TYPE/ FREQUENCY: Web site/ Daily

DESCRIPTION:
Diversity job site. Job-posting license lets employers post unlimited number of jobs themselves.

COVERAGE: Global

RATES:
1 month $125; 3 months $325; 6 months $525; 1 year $750; other options available.

RECRUITING SECTION: Professionals

AUDIENCE CHARACTERISTICS:
• College Graduates

ADVERTISING CONTACT:
Pedro Medrano
Sales
PH: (650) 962-0235
FAX: (408) 273-6467
sales@diversilink.com

Diversity Employment

Innovative Human Resources Solutions
PMB 360
801 W. El Camino Real
Mountainview, CA 94040-2511
PH: (650) 962-0235
FAX: (408) 273-6467
www.diversityemployment.com
sales@diversityemployment.com

TYPE/ FREQUENCY: Web site/ Daily

DESCRIPTION:
A multicultural employment resource offering a job and resume database. Job-posting license lets employers post unlimited number of jobs themselves.

COVERAGE: Global

RATES:
1 month $125; 3 months $325; 6 months $525; 1 year $750; other options available.

RECRUITING SECTION: General Recruitment

AUDIENCE CHARACTERISTICS:
• College Graduates

ADVERTISING CONTACT:
Sales
PH: (650) 962-0235
FAX: (408) 273-6467

DiversityRecruiting.com

Richard Clarke & Associates, Inc.
9 W. 95th St.
#C
New York, NY 10025
PH: (212) 222-5600
www.diversityrecruiting.com

TYPE/ FREQUENCY: Web site/ Daily

DESCRIPTION:
Job search web site directed at diverse audience.

COVERAGE: Global

RATES:
$100 per job per 30-day listing.

RECRUITING SECTION: Professionals

AUDIENCE CHARACTERISTICS:
• College Graduates

ADVERTISING CONTACT:
Account Representative
PH: (212) 222.5600

Dos Mundos

902-A Southwest Blvd.
Kansas City, MO 64108
PH: (816) 221-4747
FAX: (816) 221-4894
www.dosmundos.com
classifieds@dosmundos.com; adsales@dosmundos.com

TYPE/ FREQUENCY: Newspaper/ Biweekly

DESCRIPTION:
Midwest's leading bilingual newspaper.

CIRCULATION/ AUDITED BY: 700,000/ CPVS

COVERAGE: Kansas City, MO

RATES:
1-15 words $8.50; 16-22 $10.50; 23-29 $12.50; 30-36 $14.50.

RECRUITING SECTION: Professionals

AUDIENCE CHARACTERISTICS:
• Spanish Language

ADVERTISING CONTACT:
Classifieds
PH: (816) 221-4747
FAX: (816) 221-4894
classifieds@dosmundos.com

El Chicano

Inland Empire Community Newspapers
PO Box 6247
San Bernardino, CA 92412
PH: (909) 381-9898
FAX: (909) 384-0406

TYPE/ FREQUENCY: Newspaper/ Weekly

DESCRIPTION:
Community newspaper that reaches a largely Hispanic audience.

CIRCULATION/ AUDITED BY: 98,000

COVERAGE: San Bernadino, CA

RATES:
$16.90 per column inch.

RECRUITING SECTION: General Recruitment

AUDIENCE CHARACTERISTICS:
• Spanish Language

ADVERTISING CONTACT:
Kathy Boswell
Classifieds
PH: (909) 381-9898
FAX: (909) 384-0406

El Heraldo

El Heraldo Community News
1975 E. Sunrise Blvd., #810
Ft. Lauderdale, FL 33304
PH: (954) 527-0627
FAX: (954) 792-7402
www.elheraldo.com

TYPE/ FREQUENCY: Newspaper/ Weekly

DESCRIPTION:
Targets the second and third generation Latino families and business in southwest Broward County.

CIRCULATION/ AUDITED BY: 22,000

COVERAGE: Southern FL

RATES:
$30 for 5 lines; $2.00 each additional line; display ads: $10 per column inch.

RECRUITING SECTION: General Recruitment

AUDIENCE CHARACTERISTICS:
• Spanish Language

ADVERTISING CONTACT:
Classifieds
PH: (954) 963-4000.
FAX: (954) 792-7402

El Latino

El Latino Semanal/El Latino.com
4325 Georgia Ave.
West Palm Beach, FL 33405
PH: (561) 835-4913
FAX: (561) 655-5059
www.ellatino.com
sales@ellatino.com

TYPE/ FREQUENCY: Newspaper/ Weekly

DESCRIPTION:
Hispanic community newspaper serving South Florida.

CIRCULATION/ AUDITED BY: 36,000

COVERAGE: Palm Beach, FL

RATES:
$9.95 for 2 weeks.

RECRUITING SECTION: General Recruitment

AUDIENCE CHARACTERISTICS:
• Spanish Language

ADVERTISING CONTACT:
Classifieds
PH: (561) 835-4914
FAX: (561) 655-5059
sales@ellatino.com

The Forward

45 E. 33rd St., #602
New York, NY 10016
PH: (212) 889-8200
FAX: (212) 689-4255

TYPE/ FREQUENCY: Newspaper/ Weekly

DESCRIPTION:
Award-winning newspaper is targeted to a highly educated
Jewish readership.

CIRCULATION/ AUDITED BY: 50,000

COVERAGE: New York, NY

RATES:
$7 per line, minimum three lines; to advertise in English or Yiddish
editions, add 50%; to advertise in all 3 editions, add 100%.

RECRUITING SECTION: General Recruitment

AUDIENCE CHARACTERISTICS:
• Russian Language, Yiddish Language

ADVERTISING CONTACT:
Advertising
PH: (212) 889-8200
FAX: (212) 689-4255

FWA News

Financial Women's Association of New York
215 Park Ave. S, #1713
New York, NY 10003
PH: (212) 533-2141
FAX: (212) 982-3008
www.fwa.org
fwaoffice@fwa.org

TYPE/ FREQUENCY: Newsletter/ Monthly

DESCRIPTION:
FWA is a nonprofit professional organization for women in
finance and financial services.

CIRCULATION/ AUDITED BY: 1,100

COVERAGE: USA

RATES:
Free.

RECRUITING SECTION: Managers and Executives

AUDIENCE CHARACTERISTICS:
• Postgraduate Degree Holders
• Finance

ADVERTISING CONTACT:
PH: (212) 533-2141
FAX: (212) 982-3008
fwaoffice@fwa.org

FWA.org

Financial Women's Association of New York
215 Park Ave. S, #1713
New York, NY 10003
PH: (212) 533-2141
FAX: (212) 982-3008
www.fwa.org
fwaoffice@fwa.org

TYPE/ FREQUENCY: Web site/ Monthly

DESCRIPTION:
FWA is a nonprofit professional organization for women in
finance and financial services.

COVERAGE: Global

RATES:
Free.

RECRUITING SECTION: Managers and Executives

AUDIENCE CHARACTERISTICS:
• Postgraduate Degree Holders
• Finance

ADVERTISING CONTACT:
Lynette Lager
PH: (212) 533-2141
FAX: (212) 982-3008
lklager@aol.com

Gaea

Association for Women Geoscientists
University of Illinois
Dept. of Geology
1301 W. Green St.
Urbana, IL 61801
PH: (217) 367-5916
www.awg.org
ads@awg.org

TYPE/ FREQUENCY: Newsletter/ Six times per year

DESCRIPTION:
Women Geoscientists' association newsletter.

CIRCULATION/ AUDITED BY: 1,000

COVERAGE: USA

RATES:
$4 per line.

RECRUITING SECTION: Advanced Technologies

AUDIENCE CHARACTERISTICS:
• Postgraduate Degree Holders
• Higher Education
• Sciences

ADVERTISING CONTACT:
Dr. Joanne Kluessendorf
Editor
PH: (217) 367-5916
ads@awg.org

HACE Candidate Referral Service

Hispanic Alliance for Career Enhancement
14 E. Jackson Blvd., #1310
Chicago, IL 60604
PH: (312) 435-0498
FAX: (312) 435-1494
www.hace-usa.org
haceorg@enteract.com

TYPE/ FREQUENCY: Web site/ Weekly

DESCRIPTION:
Resume referral service of HACE.

CIRCULATION/ AUDITED BY: 4,000

COVERAGE: Global

RATES:
One-time professional search fee $2,000; student internship search fee $300; memberships available.

RECRUITING SECTION: Professionals

AUDIENCE CHARACTERISTICS:
• College Graduates
• Spanish Language

ADVERTISING CONTACT:
Janice Dobschuetz
Recruiting Team
PH: (312) 435-0498
FAX: (312) 435-1491

HACE Career Conference

Hispanic Alliance for Career Enhancement
14 E. Jackson Blvd., #1310
Chicago, IL 60604
PH: (312) 435-0498
FAX: (312) 435-1494
www.hace-usa.org
haceorg@enteract.com

TYPE/ FREQUENCY: Conference/ Yearly

DESCRIPTION:
Annual career conference of organization.

COVERAGE: USA

RATES:
Contact for rates.

RECRUITING SECTION: Professionals

AUDIENCE CHARACTERISTICS:
• College Graduates
• Spanish Language

ADVERTISING CONTACT:
Janice Dobschuetz
Career Conference
PH: (312) 435-0498
FAX: (312) 435-1491
haceorg@enteract.org

HACE-USA.ORG

Hispanic Alliance for Career Enhancement
14 E. Jackson Blvd.
#1310
Chicago, IL 60604
PH: (312) 435-0498
FAX: (312) 435-1494
www.hace-usa.org
haceorg@enteract.com

TYPE/ FREQUENCY: Web site/ Daily

DESCRIPTION:
HACE's mission is to provide linkage and access for Hispanic professionals to private and public organizations.

COVERAGE: Global

RATES:
Contact for rates.

RECRUITING SECTION: Professionals

AUDIENCE CHARACTERISTICS:
• College Graduates
• Spanish Language

ADVERTISING CONTACT:
Maria Elena Medina
Marketing
PH: (312) 435-0498
FAX: (312) 435-1491
memedina@hace-usa.org

HeadsUp

Black Geeks Online
122 Rhode Island Ave. NW
Washington, DC 20001-1633
PH: (202) 232-3569
www.blackgeeks.com
sistahgeek@blackgeeks.com

TYPE/ FREQUENCY: E-mail list/ Three times per week

DESCRIPTION:
Electronic bulletin of nonprofit, supporting Black computer "geeks" in all industries.

CIRCULATION/ AUDITED BY: 28,000

COVERAGE: Global

RATES:
Corporations: $50 per insertion; nonprofits, educational institutions: $30 per insertion, $75 for 3 insertions.

RECRUITING SECTION: Advanced Technologies

AUDIENCE CHARACTERISTICS:
• Advanced Technologies, Computers/Information Technology

ADVERTISING CONTACT:
Anita Brown
Founder and Chair
PH: (202) 232-3569
sistahgeek@blackgeeks.com

Hire Diversity Career Fairs

HireDiversity.com
425 Pine Ave.
Santa Barbara, CA 93117-3709
PH: (805) 964-4554
www.hirediversity.com
hd@hirediversity.com

TYPE/ FREQUENCY: Career fair/ Biannually

DESCRIPTION:
Career fairs targeting diversity audience. One fair on the East coast, one on the West.

COVERAGE: USA

RATES:
$2,500 per booth per fair.

RECRUITING SECTION: Professionals

AUDIENCE CHARACTERISTICS:
• College Graduates

ADVERTISING CONTACT:
Steven Garcia
Sales Manager
PH: (800) 810-7521 ext. 802
FAX: (805) 964-7239

HireDiversity.com

Hispanic Business.com
425 Pine Ave.
Santa Barbara, CA 93117-3709
PH: (805) 964-4554
www.hirediversity.com
hd@hirediversity.com

TYPE/ FREQUENCY: Web site/ Daily

DESCRIPTION:
Web site targeting diversity.

COVERAGE: Global

RATES:
$275 per job.

RECRUITING SECTION: Professionals

AUDIENCE CHARACTERISTICS:
• College Graduates

ADVERTISING CONTACT:
Steven Garcia
Sales Manager
PH: (800) 810-7521 ext. 802
FAX: (805) 964-7239

Hispania News

2860 S. Circle Dr., #2224
Colorado Springs, CO 80935-5116
PH: (800) 395-7804
FAX: (719) 540-0599
www.hispanianews.com
editor@hispanianews.com

TYPE/ FREQUENCY: Newspaper/ Weekly

DESCRIPTION:
Hispanic community newspaper.

CIRCULATION/ AUDITED BY: 10,000

COVERAGE: Colorado Springs, CO

RATES:
$13 per column inch.

RECRUITING SECTION: General Recruitment

AUDIENCE CHARACTERISTICS:
• Spanish Language

ADVERTISING CONTACT:
Classifieds
PH: (719) 540-0220 or 0221
FAX: (719) 540-0599

Hispanic Business Magazine

425 Pine Ave.
Santa Barbara, CA 93117-3709
PH: (805) 964-4554
www.hispanicbusiness.com

TYPE/ FREQUENCY: Magazine/ Monthly

DESCRIPTION:
Monthly magazine targeting Hispanic managers and entrepreneurs.

CIRCULATION/ AUDITED BY: 215,000/ ABC

COVERAGE: USA

RATES:
$375 per column inch.

RECRUITING SECTION: Managers and Executives

AUDIENCE CHARACTERISTICS:
• College Graduates
• Spanish Language

ADVERTISING CONTACT:
Advertising
PH: (805) 964-4554

Hispanic Career World

Equal Opportunity Publications, Inc.
445 Broad Hollow Rd., #425
Melville, NY 11747
PH: (631) 421-9421
FAX: (631) 421-0359
www.eop.com
info@eop.com

TYPE/ FREQUENCY: Magazine/ Two times per year

DESCRIPTION:
Addresses the critical shortage of IT professionals by focusing on Hispanics in technical fields.

COVERAGE: USA

RATES:
$250 per month per magazine for online editions; call for print rates.

RECRUITING SECTION: Advanced Technologies

AUDIENCE CHARACTERISTICS:
• College Graduates
• High-Tech
• Computers/Information Technology, Sciences, Engineering
• Spanish Language

ADVERTISING CONTACT:
Advertising
PH: (631) 421-9421
FAX: (631) 421-0359
info@eop.com

Hispanic Engineer and Information Technology

Career Communications Group, Inc.
729 E. Pratt St., #504
Baltimore, MD 21202
PH: (410) 244-7107
FAX: (410) 752-1834
www.ccgmag.com

TYPE/ FREQUENCY: Magazine/ Biannually

DESCRIPTION:
Targeted to Hispanic professionals and students in science and technology.

CIRCULATION/ AUDITED BY: 15,000

COVERAGE: USA

RATES:
1/2 page b/w $2,952 .

RECRUITING SECTION: Advanced Technologies

AUDIENCE CHARACTERISTICS:
• College Graduates
• High-Tech
• Sciences, Engineering
• Spanish Language

ADVERTISING CONTACT:
Advertising
PH: (410) 244-7107
FAX: (410) 752-1834

Hispanic Journal of Behavioral Sciences

Sage Publications
245 Teller Rd.
Thousand Oaks, CA 91320
PH: (805) 499-0721
FAX: (805) 499-8096
www.sagepub.com

TYPE/ FREQUENCY: Journal/ Quarterly

DESCRIPTION:
Reaches researchers, educators, mental health professionals, and sociologists interested in the latest research and analyses on Hispanic issues.

CIRCULATION/ AUDITED BY: 500

COVERAGE: International

RATES:
Contact for rates.

RECRUITING SECTION: Professionals

AUDIENCE CHARACTERISTICS:
• College Graduates
• Higher Education
• Spanish Language

ADVERTISING CONTACT:
Patricia Chojnicki
Advertising
PH: (805) 499-0721 ext. 7160
FAX: (805) 499-8096
advertising@sagepub.com

Hispanic Link Weekly Report

Hispanic Link News Service
1420 N St. NW
Washington, DC 20005
PH: (202) 234-0280
FAX: (202) 234-4090
www.hispaniclink.org

TYPE/ FREQUENCY: Newsletter/ Weekly

DESCRIPTION:
National coverage on what's happening that affects the lives and opportunities of U.S. Hispanics.

CIRCULATION/ AUDITED BY: 18,000

COVERAGE: USA

RATES:
$45 per column inch

RECRUITING SECTION: Professionals

AUDIENCE CHARACTERISTICS:
• College Graduates
• Spanish Language

ADVERTISING CONTACT:
Carlos Ericsen
Advertising
PH: (202) 234-0280
FAX: (202) 234-4090
carlos@hispaniclink.org

Hispanic Magazine

Hispanic Publishing Corporation
999 Ponce de Leon, #600
Coral Gables, FL 33134
PH: (305) 442-2462
FAX: (305) 774-3578
www.hispanicmagazine.com

TYPE/ FREQUENCY: Magazine/ Monthly

DESCRIPTION:
Magazine targeting Hispanic executives and entrepreneurs.

CIRCULATION/ AUDITED BY: 250,000/ BPA

COVERAGE: USA

RATES:
1/3 page b/w $8,235; 1/2 page $9,445.

RECRUITING SECTION: Managers and Executives

AUDIENCE CHARACTERISTICS:
• College Graduates
• Spanish Language

ADVERTISING CONTACT:
Advertising
PH: (305) 442-2462

Hispanic MBA

National Society of Hispanic MBAs
8294 Elmbrook, #235
Dallas, TX 75247
PH: (877) 467-4622
FAX: (214) 267-1626
www.nshmba.org
info@nshmba.org

TYPE/ FREQUENCY: Magazine/ Biannually

DESCRIPTION:
The official magazine of the NAHMBA reaches the Hispanic MBA membership and graduate business students.

CIRCULATION/ AUDITED BY: 15,000

COVERAGE: USA

RATES:
Full page b/w $4,765 per insertion; 1/2 page b/w $2,845 per insertion.

RECRUITING SECTION: Managers and Executives

AUDIENCE CHARACTERISTICS:
• Postgraduate Degree Holders
• Spanish Language

ADVERTISING CONTACT:
Rene Avendano
Hispanic MBA Magazine
PH: (562) 496-4428
advertisinghmba@nshmba.org

Hispanic MBA Career Fairs

National Society of Hispanic MBAs
8204 Elmbrook, #235
Dallas, TX 75247
PH: (877) 467-4622
FAX: (214) 267-1626
www.nshmba.org
info@nshmba.org

TYPE/ FREQUENCY: Career fair/ Monthly

DESCRIPTION:
Partnering with Brass Ring to offer world class events designed to allow companies to reach a diverse audience.

COVERAGE: USA

RATES:
Call for rates and schedule.

RECRUITING SECTION: Managers and Executives

AUDIENCE CHARACTERISTICS:
• College Graduates

ADVERTISING CONTACT:
Tim Marsac
Brass Ring
PH: (800) 299-7494 ext. 351
tmarsac@brassring.com

Hispanic Nurses Unnamed Journal

National Association of Hispanic Nurses
1501 16th St. NW
Washington, DC 20036
PH: (202) 387-2477
FAX: (202) 483-7183
www.thehispanicnurses.org
info@nahnhq.org

TYPE/ FREQUENCY: Journal/ Quarterly

DESCRIPTION:
Organization committed to the recruitment and retention of Hispanics into nursing and the professional development of Hispanic nurses. Journal will be new for 2002; name as yet undecided.

COVERAGE: USA

RATES:
Rates not yet established.

RECRUITING SECTION: Professionals

AUDIENCE CHARACTERISTICS:
• College Graduates
• Health Care
• Medical
• Spanish Language

ADVERTISING CONTACT:
Journal
PH: (202) 387-2477
FAX: (202) 483-7183
info@nanhq.org

Hispanic Today

E. M. Publishing Enterprises
19456 Ventura Blvd.
#200
Tarzana, CA 91356
PH: (818) 774-0870
FAX: (818) 654-0874
empei@aol.com

TYPE/ FREQUENCY: Magazine/ Quarterly

DESCRIPTION:
The publication is dedicated to informing the Hispanic community of job and career opportunities.

CIRCULATION/ AUDITED BY: 7,500

COVERAGE: USA

RATES:
Contact for rates.

RECRUITING SECTION: Professionals

AUDIENCE CHARACTERISTICS:
• College Graduates
• Spanish Language

ADVERTISING CONTACT:
Dariush Pasha
Sales Manager
PH: (818) 774-1931
FAX: (818) 654-0874

R E C R U I T I N G   T O O L S

Hispanicareers.com

Diversity Village Inc.
287 E. 6th St., #200
St. Paul, MN 55105
PH: (651) 224-0330
FAX: (651) 224-0740
www.hispanicareers.com

TYPE/ FREQUENCY: Web site/ Daily

DESCRIPTION:
Web site providing recruitment and career resources to Hispanic Americans.

COVERAGE: Global

RATES:
Contact for rates.

RECRUITING SECTION: Professionals

AUDIENCE CHARACTERISTICS:
• College Graduates
• Spanish Language

ADVERTISING CONTACT:
Omar Salas
Sales
PH: (651) 224-0330
FAX: (651) 224-0740

HispanicHealth.org

National Coalition of Hispanic Health and Human Service Organizations
1501 16th St. NW
Washington, DC 20036
PH: (202) 387-5000
FAX: (202) 797-4353
www.hispanichealth.org
info@hispanichealth.org

TYPE/ FREQUENCY: Web site/ Daily

DESCRIPTION:
Organization supporting Hispanic health and Hispanic health and social services professionals.

COVERAGE: Global

RATES:
Free.

RECRUITING SECTION: Professionals

AUDIENCE CHARACTERISTICS:
• College Graduates
• Health Care
• Medical, Social Services
• Spanish Language

ADVERTISING CONTACT:
Career Opportunities
PH: (202) 387-5000
FAX: (202) 797-4353

HispanicOnline.com

Hispanic Publishing Corporation
999 Ponce de Leon, #600
Coral Gables, FL 33134
PH: (305) 442-2462
FAX: (305) 774-3578
www.hispaniconline.com

TYPE/ FREQUENCY: Web site/ Daily

DESCRIPTION:
Premier site for Hispanics on the web. Targets Hispanic executives and entrepreneurs.

COVERAGE: Global

RATES:
Career center currently undergoing renovation; call for rates.

RECRUITING SECTION: Professionals

AUDIENCE CHARACTERISTICS:
• College Graduates
• Spanish Language

ADVERTISING CONTACT:
Blanca Recio Martinez
Sales Manager
PH: (305) 442-2462
brecio@hisp.com

HNBA.com

Hispanic National Bar Association
8201 Greensboro Dr., #300
McLean, VA 22102
PH: (703) 610-9038
FAX: (703) 610-9005
www.hnba.com
hnba@hnba.com

TYPE/ FREQUENCY: Web site/ Monthly

DESCRIPTION:
Bar association career opportunities.

COVERAGE: Global

RATES:
Private: $100 per job per 30-60 days.

RECRUITING SECTION: Professionals

AUDIENCE CHARACTERISTICS:
• Postgraduate Degree Holders
• Legal
• Spanish Language

ADVERTISING CONTACT:
Career Opportunities
PH: (703) 610-9038
FAX: (703) 610-9005
hnba@hnba.com

Houston Defender

PO Box 8005
Houston, TX 77288
PH: (713) 663-6996
FAX: (713) 663-7116

TYPE/ FREQUENCY: Newspaper/ Weekly

DESCRIPTION:
Houston's leading Black newspaper.

CIRCULATION/ AUDITED BY: 32,000/ CPVS

COVERAGE: Houston, TX

RATES:
$19.40 per column inch.

RECRUITING SECTION: General Recruitment

AUDIENCE CHARACTERISTICS:
• College Graduates

ADVERTISING CONTACT:
Stephanie Packer
PH: (713) 663-6996 ext. 112
FAX: (713) 663-7116

Iamable.net

Diversity Village Inc.
287 E. 6th St., #200
St. Paul, MN 55105
PH: (651) 224-0330
FAX: (651) 224-0740
www.iamable.net

TYPE/ FREQUENCY: Web site/ Daily

DESCRIPTION:
Web site providing recruitment and career resources to persons with disabilities.

COVERAGE: Global

RATES:
Contact for rates.

RECRUITING SECTION: Professionals

AUDIENCE CHARACTERISTICS:
• College Graduates

ADVERTISING CONTACT:
Omar Salas
Sales
PH: (651) 224-0330
FAX: (651) 224-0740

iHispano.com

20 N. Clark St., #2900
Chicago, IL 60602
PH: (312) 279-2000
FAX: (312) 346-1438
www.ihispano.com
support@ihispano.com

TYPE/ FREQUENCY: Web site/ Daily

DESCRIPTION:
Latino Internet career site.

COVERAGE: Global

RATES:
Single job posting: $135 for up to 60 days; 10 job pack: $1,100; 20 job pack: $2,000; 50 job pack: $4,250; memberships available for companies with a high volume of posting needs.

RECRUITING SECTION: General Recruitment

AUDIENCE CHARACTERISTICS:
• College Graduates
• Spanish Language

ADVERTISING CONTACT:
Customer Support
PH: (312) 346-5525
FAX: (312) 346-1438
support@ihispano.com

IMDiversity.com

iMinorities, Inc.
909 Poydras St.
36th Floor
New Orleans, LA 70112
PH: (504) 523-0154
FAX: (504) 598-3894
www.imdiversity.com
michelle@imdiversity.com

TYPE/ FREQUENCY: Web site/ Daily

DESCRIPTION:
Real-time job postings, features Asian American, African American, Hispanic American, Native American, women, and minorities' global "villages" that offer specific content.

COVERAGE: Global

RATES:
$175 per job per 60 days; also offers annual memberships with special privileges.

RECRUITING SECTION: Professionals

AUDIENCE CHARACTERISTICS:
• College Graduates

ADVERTISING CONTACT:
Michelle Ancar
Imdiversity.com
PH: (504) 523-0514 ext. 301
FAX: (504) 598-3894
michelle@imdiversity.com

India Abroad

43 W. 24th St.
New York, NY 10010
PH: (212) 929-2392
FAX: (212) 691-0873
www.indiaabroad.com
classified@indiaabroad.com

TYPE/ FREQUENCY: Newspaper/ Weekly

DESCRIPTION:
National Indian newspaper.

CIRCULATION/ AUDITED BY: 70,000

COVERAGE: USA

RATES:
Minimum $20 for 10 words; $2 each additional word; display classified: $60 for 1 column inch; rates are for local edition (East, Midwest, West; 50% surcharge to appear in all); for an additional $20, ad can be published in web addition.

RECRUITING SECTION: General Recruitment

AUDIENCE CHARACTERISTICS:
• Hindi Language

ADVERTISING CONTACT:
Classifieds
PH: (212) 929-2392
FAX: (212) 691-0873
classified@indiaabroad.com

Indian Country Today

PO Box 4250
1920 Lombardy Dr.
Rapid City, SD 57703
PH: (888) 550-1311
FAX: (605) 341-6940
www.indiancountry.com
editor@indiancountry.com

TYPE/ FREQUENCY: Newspaper/ Weekly

DESCRIPTION:
Native American newspaper.

CIRCULATION/ AUDITED BY: 15,000

COVERAGE: USA

RATES:
Classified display: $16.85 per column inch.

RECRUITING SECTION: General Recruitment

AUDIENCE CHARACTERISTICS:
• High School Graduates, College Graduates

ADVERTISING CONTACT:
Advertising
PH: (888) 550-1311
FAX: (605) 341-6940
editor@indiancountry.com

Indianapolis Recorder

2901 N. Tacoma Ave.
Indianapolis, IN 46218
PH: (317) 924-5143
FAX: (317) 924-5148
www.indianapolisrecorder.com
recorder@indy.net

TYPE/ FREQUENCY: Newspaper/ Weekly

DESCRIPTION:
African American community news.

CIRCULATION/ AUDITED BY: 13,300/ CVC

COVERAGE: Indianapolis, IN

RATES:
$14.50 per column inch.

RECRUITING SECTION: General Recruitment

AUDIENCE CHARACTERISTICS:
• High School Graduates, College Graduates

ADVERTISING CONTACT:
Sharon Maxey
Sales
PH: (317) 924-5143
FAX: (317) 924-5148
recorder@indy.net

India-West

India West
933 MacArthur Blvd.
San Leandro, CA 94577
PH: (510) 383-1143
FAX: (510) 383-1155
www.indiawest.com
classifieds@indiawest.com

TYPE/ FREQUENCY: Newspaper/ Weekly

DESCRIPTION:
North America's most honored weekly Indian newspaper.

CIRCULATION/ AUDITED BY: 30,000

COVERAGE: West Coast of CA

RATES:
$1 per word, minimum of $20.

RECRUITING SECTION: General Recruitment

AUDIENCE CHARACTERISTICS:
• Hindi Language

ADVERTISING CONTACT:
Classifieds
FAX: (510) 383-1155
classifieds@indiawest.com

Inroadsinc.org

INROADS, Inc.
10 S. Broadway, #700
St. Louis, MO 63102
PH: (314) 241-7488
FAX: (314) 241-9325
www.inroadsinc.org
info@inroadsinc.org

TYPE/ FREQUENCY: Web site/ Daily

DESCRIPTION:
Organization that sets up internships for minority and inner city students

COVERAGE: Global

RATES:
Program costs range from $3,700 to $4,200 per intern.

RECRUITING SECTION: General Recruitment

ADVERTISING CONTACT:
Local Affiliate Directory
PH: (314) 241-7488
FAX: (314) 241-9325
info@inroadsinc.org

Insight News

Marcus Garvey House
1815 Bryant Ave. N
Minneapolis, MN 55411
PH: (612) 588-1313
FAX: (612) 588-0048
www.insightnews.com
jreason@insightnews.com

TYPE/ FREQUENCY: Newspaper/ Weekly

DESCRIPTION:
African American community news.

CIRCULATION/ AUDITED BY: 35,000/ CPVS

COVERAGE: Minneapolis, MN

RATES:
Online classifieds: $25 per week.

RECRUITING SECTION: General Recruitment

AUDIENCE CHARACTERISTICS:
• High School Graduates, College Graduates

ADVERTISING CONTACT:
J. Reason
PH: (612) 588-1313
FAX: (612) 588-0048
jreason@insightnews.com

iVillage.com

iVillage
500-512 7th Ave.
New York, NY 10018
PH: (212) 600-6000
www.ivillage.com

TYPE/ FREQUENCY: Web site/ Daily

DESCRIPTION:
Premier site for women on the web. Career channel powered by CareerBuilder.com.

CIRCULATION/ AUDITED BY: 166,000,000

COVERAGE: Global

RATES:
$175 per job; packages available.

RECRUITING SECTION: General Recruitment

AUDIENCE CHARACTERISTICS:
• College Graduates

ADVERTISING CONTACT:
CareerBulider.com
PH: (888) 670-8326

IWITTS.com

Institute for Women in Trades, Technology & Science
1150 Ballena Blvd., #102
Alameda, CA 94501-3682
PH: (510) 749-0200
FAX: (510) 749-0500
www.iwitts.com
info@iwitts.com

TYPE/ FREQUENCY: Web site/ Daily

DESCRIPTION:
The number one web site for women interested in male-dominated occupations; supporting women in nontraditional jobs.

COVERAGE: Global

RATES:
$200 per year.

RECRUITING SECTION: Advanced Technologies

AUDIENCE CHARACTERISTICS:
• Computers/ Information Technology, Sciences, Advanced Technologies

ADVERTISING CONTACT:
Donna Milgram
Executive Director
PH: (510) 749-0200
FAX: (510) 749-0500
donnam@iwitts.com

Jewish Business Quarterly

E. M. Publishing Enterprises
19456 Ventura Blvd., #200
Tarzana, CA 91356
PH: (818) 774-0870
FAX: (818) 654-0874
empei@aol.com

TYPE/ FREQUENCY: Magazine/ Quarterly

DESCRIPTION:
Serves the Jewish community's goal of fostering understanding and diversity on a worldwide basis.

CIRCULATION/ AUDITED BY: 7,500

COVERAGE: USA

RATES:
Contact for rates.

RECRUITING SECTION: Professionals

AUDIENCE CHARACTERISTICS:
• College Graduates

ADVERTISING CONTACT:
Dariush Pasha
Sales Manager
PH: (818) 774-1931
FAX: (818) 654-0874

The Jewish Chronicle

5600 Baum Blvd.
Pittsburgh, PA 15206
PH: (412) 687-1000
FAX: (412) 687-5119
pittjewchr@aol.com

TYPE/ FREQUENCY: Newspaper/ Weekly

DESCRIPTION:
Newspaper targeting the Jewish community of Pittsburgh.

CIRCULATION/ AUDITED BY: 14,000

COVERAGE: Pittsburgh, PA

RATES:
$5 per 10 words; 20¢ each additional word.

RECRUITING SECTION: Managers and Executives

AUDIENCE CHARACTERISTICS:
• College Graduates

ADVERTISING CONTACT:
Advertising
PH: (412) 687-1000
FAX: (412) 687-5119
pittjewchr@aol.com

JMOJOBS.com

Midwest Military Recruiters, Inc.
1396 Windburn Dr.
Marietta, GA 30066
PH: (770) 579-4687
FAX: (770) 579-4690
www.jmojobs.com
gshook@mediaone.net

TYPE/ FREQUENCY: Web site/ Daily

DESCRIPTION:
Web site targets separating military personnel.

COVERAGE: Global

RATES:
Basic web site job posting: $75 per ad per month.

RECRUITING SECTION: General Recruitment

AUDIENCE CHARACTERISTICS:
• College Graduates, High School Graduates, Trade/ Professional
School Graduates

ADVERTISING CONTACT:
Greg Shook
PH: (770) 579-4687
FAX: (770) 579-4690
gshook@mediaone.net

Job Flash Newsletter

Women Unlimited
71 Winthrop St.
Augusta, ME 04330
PH: (800) 281-5259
FAX: (207) 623-7299
www.womenunlimited.org

TYPE/ FREQUENCY: Newsletter/ Bimonthly

DESCRIPTION:
Job opportunity newsletter sent to women looking for
employment in the construction industry.

CIRCULATION/ AUDITED BY: 800

COVERAGE: ME

RATES:
Free.

RECRUITING SECTION: General Recruitment

AUDIENCE CHARACTERISTICS:
• Construction

ADVERTISING CONTACT:
Newsletter
PH: (207) 623-7576
FAX: (207) 623-7299

Job Opportunities for the Blind

National Federation for the Blind
1800 Johnson St.
Baltimore, MD 21230
PH: (410) 659-9314
FAX: (410) 685-5653
www.nfb.org
nfb@nfb.org

TYPE/ FREQUENCY: Resource center/ Daily

DESCRIPTION:
National Federation for the Blind's new program working with
regional centers to place eligible individuals. Funded in part by a
U.S. Department of Labor grant.

COVERAGE: USA

RATES:
Free.

RECRUITING SECTION: General Recruitment

AUDIENCE CHARACTERISTICS:
• College Graduates

ADVERTISING CONTACT:
James Gashel
Director of Government Affairs
PH: (410) 659-9314
FAX: (410) 685-5653
nfb@iamdigex.net

JobAccess.org

Job Access
1001 W. 17th St.
Costa Mesa, CA 92627
PH: (949) 854-8700
FAX: (949) 548-5966
www.jobaccess.org
generalinquiries@jobaccess.org

TYPE/ FREQUENCY: Web site/ Daily

DESCRIPTION:
Working with companies, governments, and nonprofits to employ
persons with disabilities.

COVERAGE: Global

RATES:
$100 per job posting; packages available.

RECRUITING SECTION: General Recruitment

AUDIENCE CHARACTERISTICS:
• College Graduates

ADVERTISING CONTACT:
HeadHunter.net
PH: (877) 235-8978

Jobs4Women.com

WWWomen, Inc.
435 2nd Ave., #2
Attn: Jobs4Women
San Francisco, CA 94118
PH: (415) 673-0800
FAX: (415) 673-0802
www.jobs4women.com

TYPE/ FREQUENCY: E-mail list/ Weekly

DESCRIPTION:
E-mail list of job announcements from employers with openings in the Bay Area of Northern California; separate lists for different fields.

COVERAGE: San Francisco, CA

RATES:
$60 per job per list selected; $50 for nonprofit or government; $500 for corporate 10-job pak; $400 for nonprofit/government.

RECRUITING SECTION: General Recruitment

AUDIENCE CHARACTERISTICS:
• College Graduates

ADVERTISING CONTACT:
Jobs4Women
PH: (415) 673-0800
FAX: (415) 673-0802

Journal of African American Men

Transaction Publishers
Rutgers University
New Brunswick, NJ 08903
PH: (732) 445-2280
FAX: (732) 445-3138
www.transactionpublishers.com
trans@transactionpublishers.com

TYPE/ FREQUENCY: Journal/ Quarterly

DESCRIPTION:
The official journal of the National Council of African American Men, it serves as a forum for social scientists engaged in the analysis of the unique struggles and triumphs of black males.

CIRCULATION/ AUDITED BY: 400

COVERAGE: USA

RATES:
$300 full page.

RECRUITING SECTION: Professionals

AUDIENCE CHARACTERISTICS:
• College Graduates
• Higher Education

ADVERTISING CONTACT:
Advertising
PH: (732) 445-2280
FAX: (732) 445-3138
trans@transactionpublishers.com

Journal of American Ethnic History

Transaction Publishers
Rutgers University
New Brunswick, NJ 08903
PH: (732) 445-2280
FAX: (732) 445-3138
www.transactionpublishers.com
trans@transactionpublishers.com

TYPE/ FREQUENCY: Journal/ Quarterly

DESCRIPTION:
The official journal of the Immigration History Society; addresses various aspects of American immigration and ethnic history.

COVERAGE: International

RATES:
$500 full page.

RECRUITING SECTION: Professionals

AUDIENCE CHARACTERISTICS:
• College Graduates
• Higher Education

ADVERTISING CONTACT:
Advertising
PH: (732) 445-2280
FAX: (732) 445-3138
trans@transactionpublishers.com

Journal of Black Psychology

Sage Publications
245 Teller Rd.
Thousand Oaks, CA 91320
PH: (805) 499-0721
FAX: (805) 499-8096
www.sagepub.com

TYPE/ FREQUENCY: Journal/ Quarterly

DESCRIPTION:
Reaches researchers, educators, mental health professionals, and sociologists interested in the latest research and analyses on Black Psychology issues.

CIRCULATION/ AUDITED BY: 1,000

COVERAGE: International

RATES:
1/2 page $215; full page $300.

RECRUITING SECTION: Professionals

AUDIENCE CHARACTERISTICS:
• College Graduates

ADVERTISING CONTACT:
Patricia Chojnicki
Advertising
PH: (805) 499-0721 ext. 7160
FAX: (805) 499-8096
advertising@sagepub.com

Journal of Black Studies

Sage Publications
245 Teller Rd.
Thousand Oaks, CA 91320
PH: (805) 499-0721
FAX: (805) 499-8096
www.sagepub.com

TYPE/ FREQUENCY: Journal/ Bimonthly

DESCRIPTION:
A leading source for dynamic, innovative, and creative scholarly research on Black Studies.

CIRCULATION/ AUDITED BY: 800

COVERAGE: International

RATES:
1/2 page $215; full page $300.

RECRUITING SECTION: Professionals

AUDIENCE CHARACTERISTICS:
• College Graduates
• Higher Education

ADVERTISING CONTACT:
Patricia Chojnicki
Advertising
PH: (805) 499-0721 ext. 7160
FAX: (805) 499-8096
advertising@sagepub.com

Journal of the National Black Nurses Association

National Black Nurses Association
8630 Fenton St.
#330
Silver Spring, MD 20910-3803
PH: (301) 589-3200
FAX: (301) 589-3223
www.nbna.org
nbna@erols.com

TYPE/ FREQUENCY: Journal/ Biannually

DESCRIPTION:
Association supporting the advancement of Black nurses; professional journal.

CIRCULATION/ AUDITED BY: 8,500

COVERAGE: USA

RATES:
Full page $1,500; 1/2 page $750.

RECRUITING SECTION: Professionals

AUDIENCE CHARACTERISTICS:
• College Graduates
• Health Care
• Medical

ADVERTISING CONTACT:
Publications
PH: (301) 589-3200
FAX: (301) 589-3223
nbna@erols.com

La Noticia

6101 Idlewild Rd., #328
Charlotte, NC 28212
PH: (704) 568-6966
FAX: (704) 568-8936
www.lanoticia.com

TYPE/ FREQUENCY: Newspaper/ Weekly

DESCRIPTION:
Spanish Language community newspaper.

CIRCULATION/ AUDITED BY: 26,000

COVERAGE: Charlotte, NC

RATES:
1/16 page $98 per issue; 1/4 page $392 per issue (rates are b/w).

RECRUITING SECTION: General Recruitment

AUDIENCE CHARACTERISTICS:
• Spanish Language

ADVERTISING CONTACT:
Alvaro Gurdian
PH: (704) 568-6966
FAX: (704) 568-8936
carolinas@lanoticia.com

La Oferta

1376 N. 4th St.
San Jose, CA 95112
PH: (800) 336-7850
FAX: (408) 436-7861
www.laoferta.com

TYPE/ FREQUENCY: Newspaper/ Weekly

DESCRIPTION:
Hispanic community newspaper.

CIRCULATION/ AUDITED BY: 45,000/ CPVS

COVERAGE: San Mateo, CA

RATES:
$30 per column inch.

RECRUITING SECTION: General Recruitment

AUDIENCE CHARACTERISTICS:
• Spanish Language

ADVERTISING CONTACT:
Classifieds
PH: (800) 336-7850
FAX: (408) 436-7861

La Opinion

411 5th St.
Los Angeles, CA 90013
PH: (213) 622-8332
FAX: (213) 896-2374
www.laiopinion.com

TYPE/ FREQUENCY: Newspaper/ Daily

DESCRIPTION:
La Opinion is the largest Spanish language daily paper in the nation. It currently ranks as the third most read daily newspaper in Los Angeles County. Complete paper is also available online.

CIRCULATION/ AUDITED BY: 118,080/ ABC

COVERAGE: Southern CA

RATES:
Liner ads: $7 per line per day; display ads: $56 per inch per day; frequency discounts available.

RECRUITING SECTION: General Recruitment

AUDIENCE CHARACTERISTICS:
• Spanish Language

ADVERTISING CONTACT:
Fernando Jimenez
Classifieds
PH: (213) 896-2275
FAX: (213) 896-2238
classificados@laopinion.com

La Prensa

La Prensa de Minnesota
550 Concord St.
St. Paul, MN 55107
PH: (651) 224-0404
FAX: (651) 224-0098
www.laprensa-mn.com
laprensa@winternet.com

TYPE/ FREQUENCY: Newspaper/ Weekly

DESCRIPTION:
Hispanic community newspaper.

CIRCULATION/ AUDITED BY: 15,000

COVERAGE: St. Paul, MN

RATES:
$15 per column inch.

RECRUITING SECTION: General Recruitment

AUDIENCE CHARACTERISTICS:
• Spanish Language

ADVERTISING CONTACT:
Classifieds
PH: (651) 224-0404
FAX: (651) 224-0098
laprensa@winternet.com

La Prensa de San Antonio

318 S. Flores
San Antonio, TX 78204
PH: (210) 242-7900
www.laprensa.com
laprensa@hispanic.com

TYPE/ FREQUENCY: Newspaper/ Biweekly

DESCRIPTION:
Hispanic community newspaper.

CIRCULATION/ AUDITED BY: 72,000/ CPVS

COVERAGE: San Antonio, TX

RATES:
Local: $23.53 per column inch; national: $28.24 per column inch.

RECRUITING SECTION: General Recruitment

AUDIENCE CHARACTERISTICS:
• Spanish Language

ADVERTISING CONTACT:
Classifieds
PH: (210) 242-7900
laprensa@hispanic.com

La Prensa San Diego

1950 5th Ave.
San Diego, CA 92101
PH: (619) 231-2874
FAX: (619) 231-9180
www.laprensa-sandiego.org
laprensa@ix.netcom.com

TYPE/ FREQUENCY: Newspaper/ Weekly

DESCRIPTION:
Hispanic community newspaper.

CIRCULATION/ AUDITED BY: 30,000

COVERAGE: San Diego, CA

RATES:
$30.20 per column inch.

RECRUITING SECTION: General Recruitment

AUDIENCE CHARACTERISTICS:
• Spanish Language

ADVERTISING CONTACT:
Marketing Department
PH: (619) 231-2873
FAX: (619) 231-9180
laprensa@ix.netcom.com

Latin American Perspectives

Sage Publications
245 Teller Rd.
Thousand Oaks, CA 91320
PH: (805) 499-0721
FAX: (805) 499-8096
www.sagepub.com

TYPE/ FREQUENCY: Journal/ Bimonthly

DESCRIPTION:
A theoretical and scholarly journal for cross-disciplinary discussion and debate on Latin America.

CIRCULATION/ AUDITED BY: 700

COVERAGE: International

RATES:
1/2 page $215; full page $300.

RECRUITING SECTION: General Recruitment

AUDIENCE CHARACTERISTICS:
• College Graduates
• Higher Education
• Spanish Language

ADVERTISING CONTACT:
Patricia Chojnicki
Advertising
PH: (805) 499-0721 ext. 7160
FAX: (805) 499-8096
advertising@sagepub.com

Latino Law Student Job Fair

Hispanic National Bar Association
8201 Greensboro Dr., #300
McLean, VA 22102
PH: (703) 610-9038
FAX: (703) 610-9005
www.hnba.com
hnba@hnba.com

TYPE/ FREQUENCY: Career fair/ Annually

DESCRIPTION:
The largest Latino law student job fair held anywhere in the country, in conjunction with annual convention.

COVERAGE: USA

RATES:
Private employers $2,000; government $1,500; public interest $750 or $250.

RECRUITING SECTION: Professionals

AUDIENCE CHARACTERISTICS:
• Postgraduate Degree Holders
• Legal
• Spanish Language

ADVERTISING CONTACT:
Job Fair
PH: (703) 610-9038
FAX: (703) 610-9005
hnba@hnba.com

LatinoWeb Job Site

Latino Web
PO Box 3877
Montebello, CA 90640
PH: (626) 289-4443
FAX: (213) 947-1219
www.latinoweb.com
info@latinoweb.com

TYPE/ FREQUENCY: Web site/ Daily

DESCRIPTION:
General Hispanic web site.

COVERAGE: Global

RATES:
$60 for each job listing.

RECRUITING SECTION: General Recruitment

AUDIENCE CHARACTERISTICS:
• Spanish Language

ADVERTISING CONTACT:
Latino Jobs
PH: (626) 289-4443
FAX: (213) 947-1219
info@latinoweb.com

LatPro.com

LatPro, Inc.
8751 W. Broward Blvd., #404
Plantation, FL 33324
PH: (954) 474-6880 ext. 125 (advertising), ext. 114 (recruiting)
FAX: (954) 474-4760
www.latpro.com
recruiter@latpro.com; adsales@lapro.com

TYPE/ FREQUENCY: Web site/ Daily

DESCRIPTION:
LatPro.com is an award-winning site for Hispanic diversity and bilingual professionals. It is used by more than 10,000 recruiters, including 78 of the Fortune 100, to recruit the highest-caliber candidates.

CIRCULATION/ AUDITED BY: 200,000

COVERAGE: Global

RATES:
All new recruiters receive one posting free; individual job posting $125, 5-pack $500, 45-day extension $50; access to candidate database: Contact information for 20 candidates $200, full database access for 30 days $200; LatPro Plus! membership (job postings and unlimited database access for up to 5 recruiters): 1 month $500, 3 months $1,200, 6 months $2,000, 12 months $3,500.

RECRUITING SECTION: Professionals

AUDIENCE CHARACTERISTICS:
• College Graduates
• Spanish Language, Portuguese Language

ADVERTISING CONTACT:
Recruiting or Advertising
PH: (954) 474-6880 ext. 125 (advertising), ext. 114 (recruiting)
FAX: (954) 474-4760
adsales@lapro.com

Lawndale News Group

5416 W. 25th St.
Cicero, IL 60804
PH: (708) 656-6400
FAX: (708) 656-2433
www.lawndalenews.com

TYPE/ FREQUENCY: Newspaper/ Weekly

DESCRIPTION:
Hispanic community newspaper.

CIRCULATION/ AUDITED BY: 198,079/ CPVS

COVERAGE: Chicago, IL

RATES:
$45 per column inch.

RECRUITING SECTION: General Recruitment

AUDIENCE CHARACTERISTICS:
• Spanish Language

ADVERTISING CONTACT:
Classifieds
PH: (708) 656-6400
FAX: (708) 656-2433

Louisville Defender

1720 Dixie Hwy.
Louisville, KY 40210
PH: (502) 772-2591
FAX: (502) 775-8655

TYPE/ FREQUENCY: Newspaper/ Weekly

DESCRIPTION:
African American community news.

CIRCULATION/ AUDITED BY: 8,500

COVERAGE: Louisville, KY

RATES:
$9.20 per column inch.

RECRUITING SECTION: General Recruitment

AUDIENCE CHARACTERISTICS:
• High School Graduates, College Graduates

ADVERTISING CONTACT:
Classifieds
PH: (502) 772-2591
FAX: (502) 775-8655

Member Listserv

Asian American Journalist Association
1182 Market St., #320
San Francisco, CA 94102
PH: (415) 346-2051
FAX: (415) 346-6343
www.aaja.org
national@aaja.org

TYPE/ FREQUENCY: E-mail list/ Weekly

DESCRIPTION:
Professional association.

CIRCULATION/ AUDITED BY: 112,756/ BPA

COVERAGE: Global

RATES:
One week no charge on member list serve.

RECRUITING SECTION: Professionals

AUDIENCE CHARACTERISTICS:
• College Graduates
• Communications

ADVERTISING CONTACT:
Postings
PH: (415) 346-2051
FAX: (415) 346-6343
post@aaja.org

Miami County Republic

Miami County Publishing Company
121 S. Pearl
PO Box 389
Paola, KS 66071
PH: (913) 294-2311
FAX: (913) 294-5318
www.republic-online.com
republic@classicnet.net

TYPE/ FREQUENCY: Newspaper/ Biweekly

DESCRIPTION:
Rural African American community newspaper.

CIRCULATION/ AUDITED BY: 5,300

COVERAGE: Miami County, KS

RATES:
Display classified: $13.40 for Miami County marketplace; $6.70 for Monday issue.

RECRUITING SECTION: General Recruitment

AUDIENCE CHARACTERISTICS:
• High School Graduates, College Graduates

ADVERTISING CONTACT:
Heather Setter
Classifieds
PH: (913) 294-2311
FAX: (913) 294-5318
republic@classicnet.net

Michigan Chronicle

479 Ledyard St.
Detroit, MI 48201
PH: (800) 203-2229
FAX: (313) 963-8788

TYPE/ FREQUENCY: Newspaper/ Weekly

DESCRIPTION:
African American community news.

CIRCULATION/ AUDITED BY: 48,000

COVERAGE: Detroit, MI

RATES:
Display classified: $26.18 per column inch.

RECRUITING SECTION: General Recruitment

AUDIENCE CHARACTERISTICS:
• High School Graduates, College Graduates

ADVERTISING CONTACT:
Mildred Web
Advertising
PH: (313) 963-5522 ext. 239
FAX: (313) 963-8788
chronicle4@aol.com

MilitaryHeadhunter.com

Military Consulting Group
7330 Du Monde Pl.
Pensacola, FL 32505
PH: (850) 458-1416
FAX: (850) 458-1416
www.militaryheadhunter.com
customerservice@militaryheadhunter.com

TYPE/ FREQUENCY: Web site/ Daily

DESCRIPTION:
An online hiring system designed exclusively by and for military veterans.

COVERAGE: Global

RATES:
Free.

RECRUITING SECTION: General Recruitment

ADVERTISING CONTACT:
Customer Service
PH: (850) 458-1416
FAX: (850) 458-1416
customerservice@militaryheadhunter.com

The Milwaukee Times

2214 N. Martin Luther King Jr. Dr.
Milwaukee, WI 53212
PH: (414) 263-5088
FAX: (414) 863-4445
www.milwtimes.com
miltimes@execpc.com

TYPE/ FREQUENCY: Newspaper/ Weekly

DESCRIPTION:
African American community newspaper.

CIRCULATION/ AUDITED BY: 15,000/ CPVS

COVERAGE: Milwaukee, WI

RATES:
$13.50 per column inch.

RECRUITING SECTION: Professionals

ADVERTISING CONTACT:
Classifieds
PH: (414) 263-5088
FAX: (414) 263-4445
miltimes@execpc.com

Minority Engineer

Equal Opportunity Publications, Inc.
445 Broad Hollow Rd., #425
Melville, NY 11747
PH: (631) 421-9421
FAX: (631) 421-0359
www.eop.com
info@eop.com

TYPE/ FREQUENCY: Magazine/ Web site/ Three times per year

DESCRIPTION:
Distributed to the top 296 engineering schools and top MBA schools.

CIRCULATION/ AUDITED BY: 14,067/ BPA

COVERAGE: USA

RATES:
$250 per month per magazine for online editions; call for print rates.

RECRUITING SECTION: Advanced Technologies

AUDIENCE CHARACTERISTICS:
• College Graduates
• High-Tech
• Engineering

ADVERTISING CONTACT:
PH: (631) 421-9421
FAX: (631) 421-0359
info@eop.com

Minority Networking Night

The Columbus Times Newspaper
2230 Buena Vista Rd.
Columbus, GA 31907
PH: (706) 324-2404
www.columbustimes.com

TYPE/ FREQUENCY: Conference/ Monthly

DESCRIPTION:
Sponsored by the Columbus Times, a networking opportunity for minority professionals and businesses.

COVERAGE: Columbus, GA

RATES:
Free.

RECRUITING SECTION: Professionals

ADVERTISING CONTACT:
Petra Gertjegerdes-Myricks
PH: (706) 324-2404.

Modern China

Sage Publications
245 Teller Rd.
Thousand Oaks, CA 91320
PH: (805) 499-0721
FAX: (805) 499-8096
www.sagepub.com

TYPE/ FREQUENCY: Journal/ Quarterly

DESCRIPTION:
Deals with issues on China from postimperial to modern day.

CIRCULATION/ AUDITED BY: 650

COVERAGE: International

RATES:
1/2 page $215; full page $300.

RECRUITING SECTION: General Recruitment

AUDIENCE CHARACTERISTICS:
• College Graduates
• Chinese Language

ADVERTISING CONTACT:
Patricia Chojnicki
Advertising
PH: (805) 499-0721 ext. 7160
FAX: (805) 499-8096
advertising@sagepub.com

NAAAHR.org

National Association of African Americans in Human Resources
PO Box 11467
Washington, DC 20008
PH: (410) 715-8727
www.naaahr.org
naaahr@naaahr.org

TYPE/ FREQUENCY: Web site/ Weekly

DESCRIPTION:
Professional association for African Americans in human resources.

COVERAGE: Global

RATES:
$75 per month.

RECRUITING SECTION: Managers and Executives

AUDIENCE CHARACTERISTICS:
• College Graduates
• Human Resources

ADVERTISING CONTACT:
NAAAHR HR Jobs
PH: (410) 715-8727
hrjobs@naaahr.org

NAACP Career Fairs

NAACP - National Association for the Advancement of Colored People
2601 Ocean Park Blvd., #200
Santa Monica, CA 90405
PH: (310) 450-8831
FAX: (310) 396-3157
www.naacpcareerfair.com

TYPE/ FREQUENCY: Career fair/ Monthly

DESCRIPTION:
For over 20 years, NAACP career fair has been produced by Shomex Productions. It is considered the number one diversity career fair.

CIRCULATION/ AUDITED BY: 4,000

COVERAGE: USA

RATES:
Contact for rates.

RECRUITING SECTION: Professionals

AUDIENCE CHARACTERISTICS:
• College Graduates, Postgraduate Degree Holders

ADVERTISING CONTACT:
Nada McLain
Sales Department
PH: (310) 309-4417
FAX: (310) 396-3157
nmclain@shomex.com

NABA Corporate Career Center

National Association of Black Accountants
7249-A Hanover Pkwy.
Greenbelt, MD 20770
PH: (301) 474-NABA
FAX: (301) 474-3114
www.nabainc.com

TYPE/ FREQUENCY: Web site/ Daily

DESCRIPTION:
Black Accountant Association career center.

COVERAGE: Global

RATES:
Free company registration; $285 per 30-day job posting; unlimited use 1 month: $750; 1 year $5,500.

RECRUITING SECTION: Professionals

AUDIENCE CHARACTERISTICS:
• College Graduates
• Accounting

ADVERTISING CONTACT:
Career Center
PH: (301) 474-NABA
FAX: (301) 474-3114

NABJobs

National Association of Black Journalists
University of Maryland
8701-A Adelphi Rd.
Adelphi, MD 20783
PH: (301) 445-7100
FAX: (301) 445-7101
www.nabj.org

TYPE/ FREQUENCY: Web site/ Daily

DESCRIPTION:
The online career center for the National Association of Black Journalists.

COVERAGE: Global

RATES:
$150 per job posting; corporate memberships available.

RECRUITING SECTION: Professionals

AUDIENCE CHARACTERISTICS:
• College Graduates
• Communications

ADVERTISING CONTACT:
NABJobs
PH: (301) 445-7100
FAX: (301) 445-7101

NABTP.org

National Association of Black Telecommunications Professionals
1710 H St. NW
10th Floor
Washington, DC 20006
PH: (800) 946-6228
www.nabtp.org

TYPE/ FREQUENCY: Web site/ Daily

DESCRIPTION:
Promotes the professional growth and development of Blacks in the telecommunications field.

COVERAGE: Global

RATES:
Contact for rates.

RECRUITING SECTION: Advanced Technologies

AUDIENCE CHARACTERISTICS:
• College Graduates
• High-Tech
• Communications

ADVERTISING CONTACT:
PH: (800) 946-6228

NACME Journal

National Action Council for Minorities in Engineering, Inc.
Empire State Building
350 5th Ave., #2212
New York, NY 10118-2299
PH: (212) 279-2626
FAX: (212) 629-5178
www.nacme.org

TYPE/ FREQUENCY: Journal/ Annually

DESCRIPTION:
New journal for Council providing recruitment opportunities for engineers.

CIRCULATION/ AUDITED BY: 20,000

COVERAGE: USA

RATES:
Contact for rates.

RECRUITING SECTION: Advanced Technologies

AUDIENCE CHARACTERISTICS:
• College Graduates
• High-Tech
• Engineering

ADVERTISING CONTACT:
Advertising
PH: (301) 596-8808

NAHFE Annual Conference

National Association of Hispanic Federal Executives
PO Box 469
Herndon, VA 20172-0469
PH: (703) 787-0291
FAX: (703) 787-4675
www.nahfe.org
nahfe@cs.com

TYPE/ FREQUENCY: Conference/ Annually

DESCRIPTION:
Membership organization open to managers and staffers of the Federal Government at a GS-12 level or above. Annual conference has recruitment booths.

COVERAGE: USA

RATES:
Booth: $1,700.

RECRUITING SECTION: Managers and Executives

AUDIENCE CHARACTERISTICS:
• Government
• Spanish Language

ADVERTISING CONTACT:
Conference
PH: (703) 787-0291
FAX: (703) 787-4675
nahfe@cs.com

NAIW.org

National Association of Insurance Women
PO Box 4410
Tulsa, OK 74159
PH: (800) 766-6249
FAX: (918) 743-1968
www.naiw.org
joinnaiw@naiw.org

TYPE/ FREQUENCY: Web site/ Daily

DESCRIPTION:
National association promoting women in the insurance industry.

COVERAGE: Global

RATES:
$30 per ad per month; ads may be extended an additional month for $10.

RECRUITING SECTION: Professionals

AUDIENCE CHARACTERISTICS:
• College Graduates
• Insurance

ADVERTISING CONTACT:
Communications
PH: (800) 766-6249 ext. 22
FAX: (918) 743-1968
communications@naiw.org

NAJA

Native American Journalist Association
3359 36th Ave. S
Minneapolis, MN 55406
PH: (612) 729-9244
FAX: (612) 729-9373
www.naja.org
info@naja.org

TYPE/ FREQUENCY: Web site/ Weekly

DESCRIPTION:
Native American journalist professional association.

COVERAGE: Global

RATES:
Free.

RECRUITING SECTION: Professionals

AUDIENCE CHARACTERISTICS:
• College Graduates
• Communications

ADVERTISING CONTACT:
Job Bank
PH: (612) 729-9244
FAX: (612) 729-9373
info@naja.org

NAMEPA.org

National Association of Minority Engineering Program
Administrators
1133 W. Morse Blvd., #201
Winter Park, FL 32789
PH: (407) 647-8839
FAX: (407) 629-2502
www.namepa.org
nampea@namepa.org

TYPE/ FREQUENCY: Web site/ Biannually

DESCRIPTION:
Educators and representatives from industry, government, and nonprofits who share a commitment to the continued improvement of the recruitment and retention of African Americans, Latinos, and Native Americans in engineering and related fields.

COVERAGE: Global

RATES:
Contact for rates.

RECRUITING SECTION: Advanced Technologies

AUDIENCE CHARACTERISTICS:
• College Graduates
• High-Tech
• Engineering

ADVERTISING CONTACT:
NAMEPA Newsletter
PH: (407) 647-8839
FAX: (407) 629-2502
namepa@namepa.org

NAMIC

National Association of Minorities in Communication
One Centerpointe Dr., #410
La Palma, CA 90623
PH: (714) 736-9600
FAX: (714) 736-9699
www.namic.com

TYPE/ FREQUENCY: Web site/ Daily

DESCRIPTION:
NAMIC educates, advocates, and empowers for the cause of diversity in the telecommunications industry.

COVERAGE: Global

RATES:
Free.

RECRUITING SECTION: Advanced Technologies

AUDIENCE CHARACTERISTICS:
• College Graduates
• High-Tech
• Communications

ADVERTISING CONTACT:
Job Bank
PH: (410) 884-3222
FAX: (815) 425-0646
mjwesley@earthlink.net

NAPALSA.org

National Asian Pacific American Law Student Association
11918 Amblewood Dr.
Stafford, TX 77477
PH: (713) 837-9036
www.napalsa.org
napalsa@napalsa.org

TYPE/ FREQUENCY: Web site/ Daily

DESCRIPTION:
National student association has career page on web site.

COVERAGE: Global

RATES:
Free.

RECRUITING SECTION: General Recruitment

AUDIENCE CHARACTERISTICS:
- College Graduates
- Legal

ADVERTISING CONTACT:
Deborah Chen
Positions
PH: (713) 837-9036
positions@napalsa.org

NAPMW

National Association of Professional Mortgage Women
PO Box 2016
Edmonds, WA 98020-9516
PH: (800) 827-3034; (425) 778-6162
FAX: (425) 771-9588
www.napmw.org
napmw@aol.com

TYPE/ FREQUENCY: Web site/ Daily

DESCRIPTION:
Members-only job bank.

COVERAGE: Global

RATES:
$50 per listing per month.

RECRUITING SECTION: Professionals

AUDIENCE CHARACTERISTICS:
- Finance

ADVERTISING CONTACT:
Job Bank
PH: (425) 778-6162
FAX: (425) 771-9588
napmw@aol.com

NASBE.org

National Alliance of Black School Educators
310 Pennsylvania Ave. SE
Washington, DC 20003
PH: (202) 608-6310
FAX: (202) 608-6319
www.nasbe.org
nasbe@nasbe.org

TYPE/ FREQUENCY: Web site/ Daily

DESCRIPTION:
Organization dedicated to the support of Black educators.

COVERAGE: Global

RATES:
Free.

RECRUITING SECTION: Professionals

AUDIENCE CHARACTERISTICS:
- College Graduates
- Higher Education

ADVERTISING CONTACT:
Brenda
Jobs
brenda@ndgphoenix.com

NASPHQ.com

National Association of Securities Professionals
1212 New York Ave. NW, #210
Washington, DC 20005-3987
PH: (202) 371-5535
FAX: (202) 371-5536
www.nasphq.com
nasphq@aol.com

TYPE/ FREQUENCY: Web site/ Daily

DESCRIPTION:
Association was formed to expand the presence and influence of women and minorities in the securities industry.

COVERAGE: Global

RATES:
Contact for rates.

RECRUITING SECTION: Professionals

AUDIENCE CHARACTERISTICS:
- College Graduates
- Investment

ADVERTISING CONTACT:
Futures and Options Jobs Bulletin
PH: (202) 371-5535
FAX: (202) 371-5536
nasphq@aol.com

NATEA

North American Taiwanese Engineer Association
PO Box 2772
Sunnyvale, CA 94087
PH: (408) 354-8139
FAX: (408) 354-8639
www.natea.org
natea@natea.org

TYPE/ FREQUENCY: Web site/ Monthly

DESCRIPTION:
Engineering association.

CIRCULATION/ AUDITED BY: 600

COVERAGE: Global

RATES:
Sponsorship: Diamond $2,000; Platinum $1,000; allow unlimited job postings.

RECRUITING SECTION: Advanced Technologies

AUDIENCE CHARACTERISTICS:
• College Graduates
• High-Tech
• Computers/Information Technology, Engineering
• Chinese Language

ADVERTISING CONTACT:
Sponsorship
PH: (408) 354-8139
FAX: (408) 354-8639
natea@natea.org

National Association of Hispanic Nurses Annual Conference

National Association of Hispanic Nurses
1501 16th St. NW
Washington, DC 20036
PH: (202) 387-2477
FAX: (202) 483-7183
www.thehispanicnurses.org
info@nahnhq.org

TYPE/ FREQUENCY: Conference/ Annually

DESCRIPTION:
Organization committed to the recruitment and retention of Hispanics into nursing and the professional development of Hispanic nurses. Annual conference.

CIRCULATION/ AUDITED BY: 4,000

COVERAGE: USA

RATES:
Contact for rates.

RECRUITING SECTION: Professionals

AUDIENCE CHARACTERISTICS:
• College Graduates
• Health Care
• Medical
• Spanish Language

ADVERTISING CONTACT:
Conference
PH: (202) 387-2477
FAX: (202) 483-7183
info@nanhq.org

National Association of Negro Business and Professional Womens Clubs Job Line

National Association of Negro Business and Professional Women's Clubs
1806 New Hampshire Ave. NW
Washington, DC 20009
PH: (202) 483-4206

TYPE/ FREQUENCY: Phone line/ Weekly

DESCRIPTION:
Telephone job listings.

COVERAGE: USA

RATES:
Free.

RECRUITING SECTION: Professionals

ADVERTISING CONTACT:
Job Line
PH: (202) 483-4206

National Black MBA Career Fairs

National Black MBA Association
180 N. Michigan Ave., #1400
Chicago, IL 60601
PH: (312) 236-2622
FAX: (312) 236-4131
www.nbmbaa.org
mail@nbmbaa.org

TYPE/ FREQUENCY: Career fair/ Monthly

DESCRIPTION:
Partnering with Brass Ring to offer world class events designed to allow companies to reach a diverse audience.

COVERAGE: USA

RATES:
Call for rates and schedule.

RECRUITING SECTION: Managers and Executives

AUDIENCE CHARACTERISTICS:
• College Graduates

ADVERTISING CONTACT:
Tim Marsac
Brass Ring
PH: (800) 299-7494 ext. 351
tmarsac@brassring.com

National Black MBA Job Posting System

National Black MBA Association
180 N. Michigan Ave., #1400
Chicago, IL 60601
PH: (312) 236-2622
FAX: (312) 236-4131
www.nbmbaa.org
mail@nbmbaa.org

TYPE/ FREQUENCY: Web site/ Daily

DESCRIPTION:
Web site's job board making opportunities available to the African American professional market. Powered by Brass Ring.

COVERAGE: Global

RATES:
Single posting $100; packages available.

RECRUITING SECTION: Managers and Executives

AUDIENCE CHARACTERISTICS:
• Postgraduate Degree Holders

ADVERTISING CONTACT:
Tim Marsac
Brass Ring
PH: (800) 299-7494 ext. 351
tmarsac@brassring.com

National Conference

National Black MBA Association
180 N. Michigan Ave., #1400
Chicago, IL 60601
PH: (312) 236-2622
FAX: (312) 236-4131
www.nbmbaa.org
mail@nbmbaa.org

TYPE/ FREQUENCY: Conference/ Annually

DESCRIPTION:
National association's annual conference.

COVERAGE: USA

RATES:
Call for rates and schedule.

RECRUITING SECTION: Managers and Executives

AUDIENCE CHARACTERISTICS:
• Postgraduate Degree Holders

ADVERTISING CONTACT:
Convention
PH: (312) 236-2622
FAX: (312) 236-4131
mail@nbmbaa.org

Native American Times

PO Box 692050
Tulsa, OK 74169
PH: (918) 438-6548
FAX: (918) 438-6545
www.okit.com

TYPE/ FREQUENCY: Newspaper/ Monthly

DESCRIPTION:
Native American newspaper.

CIRCULATION/ AUDITED BY: 36,000

COVERAGE: OK

RATES:
$12 per column inch.

RECRUITING SECTION: General Recruitment

AUDIENCE CHARACTERISTICS:
• High School Graduates, College Graduates

ADVERTISING CONTACT:
Jim Gray
Advertising
PH: (918) 438-6548
FAX: (918) 438-6545

NativeAmericanJobs.com

PO Box 1475
Klamath Falls, OR 97601-0080
PH: (541) 273-0258
FAX: (541) 273-0258
www.nativeamericanjobs.com
jc@nativeamericanjobs.com

TYPE/ FREQUENCY: Web site/ Weekly

DESCRIPTION:
Web site targeted to Native Americans.

COVERAGE: Global

RATES:
$50 per job; annual subscriptions start at $500.

RECRUITING SECTION: General Recruitment

AUDIENCE CHARACTERISTICS:
• College Graduates, High School Graduates, Trade/Professional
  School Graduates

ADVERTISING CONTACT:
Job Posting
PH: (541) 273-0258
FAX: (541) 273-0258
jc@nativeamericanjobs.com

NativeJobs.com

Tribal Employment Newsletter
13 Briarwood Ln.
Portland, ME 04103
PH: (207) 780-1420
FAX: (207) 780-1420
www.nativejobs.com
careers@nativejobs.com

TYPE/ FREQUENCY: Web site/ Daily

DESCRIPTION:
Widely accessed Native American job site.

CIRCULATION/ AUDITED BY: 2,000 per month

COVERAGE: Global

RATES:
$80 per announcement; annual subscription available.

RECRUITING SECTION: General Recruitment

AUDIENCE CHARACTERISTICS:
• College Graduates

ADVERTISING CONTACT:
Careers
PH: (207) 780-1420
FAX: (207) 780-1420
careers@nativejobs.com

NAWIC Career Center

National Association of Women in Construction
327 S. Adams St.
Fort Worth, TX 76104-1081
PH: (817) 877-5551
FAX: (817) 877-0324
www.nawic.org
nawic@nawic.org

TYPE/ FREQUENCY: Web site/ Daily

DESCRIPTION:
National association supporting and encouraging women in the
construction industry.

COVERAGE: Global

RATES:
Classifieds: $2,50 per word for the first 10 words; $2 per
additional word; display rates available.

RECRUITING SECTION: General Recruitment

AUDIENCE CHARACTERISTICS:
• Trade/Professional School Graduates
• Construction

ADVERTISING CONTACT:
Kara Roberson
PH: (800) 552-3506 ext. 24
FAX: (817) 877-0324
karar@nawic.org

NAWIC Image

National Association of Women in Construction
327 S. Adams St.
Fort Worth, TX 76104-1081
PH: (817) 877-5551
FAX: (817) 877-0324
www.nawic.org
nawic@nawic.org

TYPE/ FREQUENCY: Magazine/ Bimonthly

DESCRIPTION:
National association supporting and encouraging women in the
construction industry.

COVERAGE: USA

RATES:
Classifieds: $2.50 per word for first 10 words; $2 each additional
word; display rates available.

RECRUITING SECTION: General Recruitment

AUDIENCE CHARACTERISTICS:
• Trade/ Professional School Graduates
• Construction

ADVERTISING CONTACT:
Kara Roberson
PH: (800) 552-3506 ext. 24
FAX: (817) 877-0324
karar@nawic.org

NBNA Conference

National Black Nurses Association
8630 Fenton St., #330
Silver Spring, MD 20910-3803
PH: (301) 589-3200
FAX: (301) 589-3223
www.nbna.org
nbna@erols.com

TYPE/ FREQUENCY: Conference/ Annually

DESCRIPTION:
Association supporting the advancement of Black nurses; annual conference.

COVERAGE: USA

RATES:
$1,000 per booth.

RECRUITING SECTION: Professionals

AUDIENCE CHARACTERISTICS:
• College Graduates
• Health Care
• Medical

ADVERTISING CONTACT:
Conference
PH: (301) 589-3200
FAX: (301) 589-3223
nbna@erols.com

NBNA Newsletter

National Black Nurses Association
8630 Fenton St., #330
Silver Spring, MD 20910-3803
PH: (301) 589-3200
FAX: (301) 589-3223
www.nbna.org
nbna@erols.com

TYPE/ FREQUENCY: Newsletter/ Quarterly

DESCRIPTION:
Association supporting the advancement of Black nurses; official newsletter.

CIRCULATION/ AUDITED BY: 6,000

COVERAGE: USA

RATES:
Full page $600; 1/2 page $325.

RECRUITING SECTION: Professionals

AUDIENCE CHARACTERISTICS:
• College Graduates
• Health Care
• Medical

ADVERTISING CONTACT:
Publications
PH: (301) 589-3200
FAX: (301) 589-3223
nbna@erols.com

NBPRS.com

National Black Public Relations Society
6565 Sunset Blvd., #301
Hollywood, CA 90028
PH: (323) 466-8221
FAX: (323) 856-9510
www.nbprs.org
nbprs@aol.com

TYPE/ FREQUENCY: Web site/ Weekly

DESCRIPTION:
The National Black Public Relations Society was established to benefit top PR and affiliated services professionals.

COVERAGE: Global

RATES:
Contact for rates.

RECRUITING SECTION: Professionals

AUDIENCE CHARACTERISTICS:
• College Graduates
• Communications

ADVERTISING CONTACT:
Trenae Floyd
Career Center
PH: (305) 651-8388
FAX: (305) 651-6651
trenaef@aol.com; vonmultimedia@aol.com

NCOJobs.com

Midwest Military Recruiters, Inc.
1396 Windburn Dr.
Marietta, GA 30066
PH: (770) 579-4687
FAX: (770) 579-4690
www.ncojobs.com
gshook@mediaone.net

TYPE/ FREQUENCY: Web site/ Daily

DESCRIPTION:
Web site targets separating military personnel—specifically NCOs.

COVERAGE: Global

RATES:
Basic web site job posting: $75 per ad per month.

RECRUITING SECTION: General Recruitment

AUDIENCE CHARACTERISTICS:
• College Graduates, High School Graduates, Trade/Professional
  School Graduates

ADVERTISING CONTACT:
Greg Shook
PH: (770) 579-4687
FAX: (770) 579-4690
gshook@mediaone.net

NDNJB

The National Diversity Newspaper Job Bank
One Riverside Ave.
Jacksonville, FL 32202
PH: (904) 359-4398
FAX: (904) 359-4695
www.newsjobs.com
newsjobs@newsjobs.com

TYPE/ FREQUENCY: Web site/ Daily

DESCRIPTION:
The National Diversity newspaper job bank is one of the nation's
most comprehensive newspaper, information, and media job
listing web sites. The NDNJB is devoted to diversifying the
industry.

CIRCULATION/ AUDITED BY: 80,924

COVERAGE: Global

RATES:
Free for job listings.

RECRUITING SECTION: Professionals

AUDIENCE CHARACTERISTICS:
• College Graduates
• Communications

ADVERTISING CONTACT:
Heather Lee Holman
NDNJB Coordinator
PH: (904) 359-4398
FAX: (904) 359-4695
newsjobs@newsjobs.com

Nemnet

The National Employment Minority Network
PO Box 30
New Haven, CT 06501
PH: (800) 694-0534
FAX: (888) 521-3838
www.nemnet.com
info@nemnet.com

TYPE/ FREQUENCY: E-mail list/ Weekly

DESCRIPTION:
A direct e-mail service that is delivered every Tuesday morning to
a diverse readership of students and professionals of color.

CIRCULATION/ AUDITED BY: 2,000

COVERAGE: Global

RATES:
Single direct listing: $125 per listing.

RECRUITING SECTION: Professionals

AUDIENCE CHARACTERISTICS:
• College Graduates, College Students, Recent Graduates

ADVERTISING CONTACT:
Advertising
PH: (800) 964-0534
FAX: (888) 521-3838
advertise@nemnet.com

Nemnet

The National Employment Minority Network
PO Box 30
New Haven, CT 06501
PH: (800) 964-0534
FAX: (888) 521-3838
www.nemnet.com
info@nemnet.com

TYPE/ FREQUENCY: Web site/ Daily

DESCRIPTION:
Nemnet is a national resource organization committed to
assisting schools and organizations in the identification and
recruitment of minority students and professionals. Web site has
job postings.

COVERAGE: Global

RECRUITING TOOLS

RATES:
$90 per listing.

RECRUITING SECTION: Professionals

AUDIENCE CHARACTERISTICS:
• College Graduates, College Students, Recent Graduates

ADVERTISING CONTACT:
Advertising
PH: (800) 964-0534
FAX: (888) 521-3838
advertise@nemnet.com

Nemnet

The National Employment Minority Network
PO Box 30
New Haven, CT 06501
PH: (800) 694-0534
FAX: (888) 521-3838
www.nemnet.com
info@nemnet.com

TYPE/ FREQUENCY: Career fair/ Varied

DESCRIPTION:
Nemnet is a national resource organization committed to assisting schools and organizations in the identification and recruitment of minority students and professionals.

COVERAGE: USA

RATES:
Contact for rates.

RECRUITING SECTION: Professionals

AUDIENCE CHARACTERISTICS:
• College Graduates, College Students, Recent Graduates

ADVERTISING CONTACT:
Career Fairs
PH: (800) 964-0534
FAX: (888) 521-3838
careerfairs@nemnet.com

NetNoir.com

Chapman Network Inc.
401 E. Pratt St.
Baltimore, MD 21202
PH: (800) 752-1013
FAX: (410) 625-9313
www.netnoir.com

TYPE/ FREQUENCY: Web site/ Daily

DESCRIPTION:
Web portal targeted to African Americans; includes a career center.

COVERAGE: Global

RATES:
$100 per job for 15 days; $180 for 30 days; $260 for 45 days.

RECRUITING SECTION: Professionals

AUDIENCE CHARACTERISTICS:
• College Graduates

ADVERTISING CONTACT:
Michael Clark
Sales
PH: (718) 636-6332
michaelclark@netnoir.net

Network

International Women's Writing Guild
Box 810 Gracie Station
New York, NY 10028
PH: (212) 737-7536
FAX: (212) 737-9469
www.iwwg.com

TYPE/ FREQUENCY: Newsletter/ Bimonthly

DESCRIPTION:
A newsletter for women writers.

CIRCULATION/ AUDITED BY: 4,000

COVERAGE: International

RATES:
60¢ per word.

RECRUITING SECTION: Professionals

AUDIENCE CHARACTERISTICS:
• College Graduates
• Communications

ADVERTISING CONTACT:
Tatiana
Editor
PH: (212) 737-7536
FAX: (212) 737-9469

New Pittsburgh Courier

315 E. Carson St.
Pittsburgh, PA 15219
PH: (412) 481-8302
FAX: (412) 481-1360

TYPE/ FREQUENCY: Newspaper/ Biweekly

DESCRIPTION:
African American community news.

COVERAGE: Pittsburgh, PA

RATES:
For single day insertion: $16.54 per column inch; for consecutive insertions: $24.27 per column inch.

RECRUITING SECTION: General Recruitment

AUDIENCE CHARACTERISTICS:
• College Graduates, High School Graduates, Trade/Professional School Graduates

ADVERTISING CONTACT:
Classifieds
PH: (412) 481-8302
FAX: (412) 481-1360
npcourier@aol.com

News from Indian Country

7831 N. Grandstone Ave.
Hayward, WI 54843
PH: (715) 634-1429
FAX: (715) 634-3243
www.indiancountrynews.com

TYPE/ FREQUENCY: Newspaper/ Bimonthly

DESCRIPTION:
Native American newspaper.

CIRCULATION/ AUDITED BY: 72,000

COVERAGE: USA

RATES:
Job ads: $17 per column inch.

RECRUITING SECTION: General Recruitment

AUDIENCE CHARACTERISTICS:
• High School Graduates, College Graduates

ADVERTISING CONTACT:
Kimberlie R. Hall
Advertising
PH: (715) 634-1429
FAX: (715) 634-3243
nficad@cheqnet.com

News from Native California

PO Box 9145
Berkeley, CA 94709
PH: (510) 549-3564
FAX: (510) 549-1889
news@heydaybooks.com

TYPE/ FREQUENCY: Magazine/ Quarterly

DESCRIPTION:
Native American publication.

CIRCULATION/ AUDITED BY: 5,000

COVERAGE: CA

RATES:
$380 per 1/2 page; $250 per 1/3 page.

RECRUITING SECTION: General Recruitment

AUDIENCE CHARACTERISTICS:
• High School Graduates, College Graduates

ADVERTISING CONTACT:
Advertising
PH: (510) 549-3564
FAX: (510) 549-1889
news@heydaybooks.com

NFB Jobline

National Federation for the Blind
1800 Johnson St.
Baltimore, MD 21230
PH: (410) 659-9314
FAX: (410) 685-5653
www.nfb.org
nfb@nfb.org

TYPE/ FREQUENCY: Telephone line

DESCRIPTION:
National Federation for the Blind's job line service.

COVERAGE: USA

RATES:
Free.

RECRUITING SECTION: General Recruitment

AUDIENCE CHARACTERISTICS:
• College Graduates

ADVERTISING CONTACT:
James Gashel
Director of Government Affairs
PH: (410) 659-9314
FAX: (410) 685-5653
jgashel@nfb.org

NHBA.org

National Hispanic Business Association
1712 E. Riverside Dr., #208
Austin, TX 78741
PH: (512) 495-9511
FAX: (512) 495-9730
www.nhba.org
vanessa@nhba.org

TYPE/ FREQUENCY: Web site/ Daily

DESCRIPTION:
Association made up of Hispanic students and alumni to address business issues related to Hispanics. Web site has job listings.

COVERAGE: Global

RATES:
Contact for rates.

RECRUITING SECTION: Professionals

AUDIENCE CHARACTERISTICS:
• College Graduates
• Spanish Language

ADVERTISING CONTACT:
Vanessa
Job Listings
PH: (512) 495-9511
FAX: (512) 495-9730
vanessa@nhba.org

NHCC-HQ.org

National Hispanic Corporate Council
1911 N. Fort Myer Dr.
Arlington, VA 22201
PH: (703) 807-5137
FAX: (703) 807-0567
www.nhcc-hq.org
csoto@nhcc-hq.org

TYPE/ FREQUENCY: Web site/ Daily

DESCRIPTION:
Association supporting Hispanic corporate leaders. Has a very high level membership and will only accept jobs at management level and higher.

COVERAGE: Global

RATES:
Free job postings, but postings must be approved.

RECRUITING SECTION: Managers and Executives

AUDIENCE CHARACTERISTICS:
• College Graduates
• Spanish Language

ADVERTISING CONTACT:
Carlos Soto
PH: (703) 807-5137
FAX: (703) 807-0567
csoto@nhcc-hq.org

Nikkei West

PO Box 2118
Cupertino, CA 95015
PH: (408) 998-0920
FAX: (978) 477-0213
www.nikkeiwest.com
mail@nikkeiwest.com

TYPE/ FREQUENCY: Newspaper/ Biweekly

DESCRIPTION:
A Japanese American community biweekly serving Northern California.

CIRCULATION/ AUDITED BY: 90,000

COVERAGE: Northern CA

RATES:
Classifieds: $15 per column inch per insertion.

RECRUITING SECTION: General Recruitment

AUDIENCE CHARACTERISTICS:
• Japanese Language

ADVERTISING CONTACT:
Classifieds
PH: (408) 998-0920 x 4916
FAX: (978) 477-0213
mail@nikkeiwest.com

NOBCChE.org

National Organization for the Professional Advancement of Black Chemists and Chemical Engineers
National Office
PO Box 77040
Washington, DC 20013
www.nobcche.org
info@nobcche.org

TYPE/ FREQUENCY: Web site/ Daily

DESCRIPTION:
Organization provides a forum for Black chemists and chemical engineers to discuss issues relevant to their careers.

COVERAGE: Global

RATES:
Job tokens (allow for posting of jobs): 1-2 jobs $200 each; 3+ jobs $100 per job.

RECRUITING SECTION: Advanced Technologies

AUDIENCE CHARACTERISTICS:
• College Graduates
• Sciences, Engineering

ADVERTISING CONTACT:
Postings Managed Online
info@nobcche.org

NOMA.net

National Organization of Minority Architects
5530 Wisconsin Ave., #1210
Chevy Chase, MD 20815
PH: (301) 941-1065
www.noma.net
avery@noma.net

TYPE/ FREQUENCY: Web site/ Daily

DESCRIPTION:
Association supporting minorities in the architectural field.

COVERAGE: Global

RATES:
$150 for 1-6 lines; $250 for 7-10 lines; $375 for 11-15 lines; $500 for 16+ lines.

RECRUITING SECTION: Professionals

AUDIENCE CHARACTERISTICS:
• College Graduates
• Architecture

ADVERTISING CONTACT:
Job Bank
PH: (301) 941-1065
avery@noma.net

NSBE Bridge

National Society of Black Engineers
1454 Duke St.
Alexandria, VA 22314
PH: (703) 549-2207
www.nsbe.org
info@nsbe.org

TYPE/ FREQUENCY: Magazine/ Three times per year

DESCRIPTION:
The premier organization linking Black engineers and the African American community to technology and opportunities. One of its official publications. Targeted at minority middle and high school students to study and succeed in engineering, science, and technology.

CIRCULATION/ AUDITED BY: 140,000

COVERAGE: USA

RATES:
$8,500 b/w full page per issue.

RECRUITING SECTION: Advanced Technologies

AUDIENCE CHARACTERISTICS:
• College Graduates
• High-Tech
• Engineering, Sciences

ADVERTISING CONTACT:
K. Harris
Advertising
PH: (703) 549-2207
kharris@nsbe.org

NSBE Magazine

National Society of Black Engineers
1454 Duke St.
Alexandria, VA 22314
PH: (703) 549-2207
www.nsbe.org
info@nsbe.org

TYPE/ FREQUENCY: Magazine/ Five times per year

DESCRIPTION:
The premier organization linking Black engineers and the African American community to technology and opportunities. One of its official publications.

CIRCULATION/ AUDITED BY: 10,000

COVERAGE: USA

RATES:
Contact for rates.

RECRUITING SECTION: Advanced Technologies

AUDIENCE CHARACTERISTICS:
- High School Graduates, College Graduates
- High-Tech
- Engineering, Sciences

ADVERTISING CONTACT:
K. Harris
Advertising
PH: (703) 549-2207
kharris@nsbe.org

NSBE National Conference

National Society of Black Engineers
1454 Duke St.
Alexandria, VA 22314
PH: (703) 549-2207
www.nsbe.org
info@nsbe.org

TYPE/ FREQUENCY: Conference/ Annually

DESCRIPTION:
The premier organization linking Black engineers and the African American community to technology and opportunities. Annual conference of its 10,000 members.

COVERAGE: USA

RATES:
Program advertising rates: 1/2 page horizontal b/w $3,874; contact for booth rates.

RECRUITING SECTION: Advanced Technologies

AUDIENCE CHARACTERISTICS:
- College Graduates
- High-Tech
- Engineering, Sciences

ADVERTISING CONTACT:
K. Harris
Advertising
PH: (703) 549-2207
kharris@nsbe.org

NSBP.org

National Society of Black Physicists
Department of Physics
North Carolina A&T State University
c/o Administrative Executive Officer
Greensboro, NC 27411-1086
PH: (336) 334-7646
FAX: (336) 334-7283
www.nsbp.org

TYPE/ FREQUENCY: E-mail list/ Daily

DESCRIPTION:
Promotes the professional well-being and increase in numbers of Black physicists. Positions sent out via listserve after approval.

COVERAGE: Global

RATES:
Free, but subject to approval.

RECRUITING SECTION: Advanced Technologies

AUDIENCE CHARACTERISTICS:
- College Graduates, Postgraduate Degree Holders
- Higher Education
- Sciences

ADVERTISING CONTACT:
NSBP Net
PH: (336) 334-7646
FAX: (336) 334-7283
nsbpnet@nsbp.org

NSHMBA.org

National Society of Hispanic MBAs
8204 Elmbrook
#235
Dallas, TX 75247
PH: (877) 467-4622
FAX: (214) 267-1626
www.nshmba.org
info@nshmba.org

TYPE/ FREQUENCY: Web site/ Daily

DESCRIPTION:
Web site's job board making opportunities available to the Hispanic professional market. Powered by Brass Ring.

COVERAGE: Global

RATES:
Single posting $100; packages available.

RECRUITING SECTION: Managers and Executives

AUDIENCE CHARACTERISTICS:
- Postgraduate Degree Holders
- Spanish Language

ADVERTISING CONTACT:
Tim Marsac
Brass Ring
PH: (800) 299-7494 ext. 351
tmarsac@brassring.com

NW Asian Weekly

Northwest Asian Weekly
PO Box 3468
Seattle, WA 98114
PH: (206) 223-5559
FAX: (206) 223-0626
www.nwasianweekly.com
scpnwan@nwlink.com

TYPE/ FREQUENCY: Newspaper/ Weekly

DESCRIPTION:
Asian American community newspaper.

CIRCULATION/ AUDITED BY: 25,000

COVERAGE: CA, WA, OR

RATES:
Classifieds: $25 for 4 lines; $5 each additional line.

RECRUITING SECTION: General Recruitment

ADVERTISING CONTACT:
Monica
Classifieds
PH: (206) 223-0623
FAX: (206) 223-0626
scpnwan@nwlink.com

Ojibwe Akiing

7831 N. Grandstone Ave.
Hayward, WI 54843
PH: (715) 634-5226
FAX: (715) 634-3243

TYPE/ FREQUENCY: Newspaper/ Weekly

DESCRIPTION:
Native American newspaper.

CIRCULATION/ AUDITED BY: 5,000

COVERAGE: WI, MN, MI

RATES:
Job ads: $10.50 per column inch.

RECRUITING SECTION: General Recruitment

AUDIENCE CHARACTERISTICS:
• High School Graduates, College Graduates

ADVERTISING CONTACT:
Trace DeMeyer
Advertising
PH: (715) 634-5226
FAX: (715) 634-3243

Oklahoma Eagle

624 E. Archer
Tulsa, OK 74120
PH: (918) 582-7124
FAX: (918) 582-8905

TYPE/ FREQUENCY: Newspaper/ Weekly

DESCRIPTION:
African American community newspaper.

CIRCULATION/ AUDITED BY: 35,000

COVERAGE: OK

RATES:
$14.80 per column inch.

RECRUITING SECTION: General Recruitment

AUDIENCE CHARACTERISTICS:
• High School Graduates, College Graduates

ADVERTISING CONTACT:
Stephanie Wolfe
Classified Advertising
PH: (918) 582-7124
FAX: (918) 582-8905

Omaha Star

The Omaha Star, Inc.
2216 N. 24th St.
PO Box 11128
Omaha, NE 68111
PH: (402) 346-4041
FAX: (402) 346-4064

TYPE/ FREQUENCY: Newspaper/ Weekly

DESCRIPTION:
The only Black newspaper in Nebraska.

CIRCULATION/ AUDITED BY: 30,000

COVERAGE: NE

RATES:
$13.58 per column inch.

RECRUITING SECTION: General Recruitment

AUDIENCE CHARACTERISTICS:
• High School Graduates, College Graduates

ADVERTISING CONTACT:
Preston Love
Advertising
PH: (402) 346-4041
FAX: (402) 346-4064

OpportunityBlvd.com

Sacramento Observer
2330 Alhambra Blvd.
Sacramento, CA 95817
PH: (916) 452-4781
www.opportunityblvd.com
info@sacobserver.com

TYPE/ FREQUENCY: Web site/ Daily

DESCRIPTION:
Sponsored by the Sacramento Observer, a job web site for the Sacramento area.

COVERAGE: Global

RATES:
$300 per month.

RECRUITING SECTION: General Recruitment

AUDIENCE CHARACTERISTICS:
• High School Graduates, College Graduates

ADVERTISING CONTACT:
Advertising
PH: (916) 452-4781
FAX: (916) 452-7744
advertise@sacobserver.com

PICKDiversity Career Fair

PICKDiversity
PO Box 696
Solvang, CA 93464
PH: (805) 688-2488
FAX: (805) 686-1570
www.pickdiversity.com
info@pickdiversity.com

TYPE/ FREQUENCY: Career fair/ Quarterly

DESCRIPTION:
Job fairs directed at diverse audiences.

COVERAGE: USA

RATES:
$2,500 per event.

RECRUITING SECTION: Professionals

AUDIENCE CHARACTERISTICS:
• College Graduates

ADVERTISING CONTACT:
Sales Department
PH: (805) 688-2488
FAX: (805) 686-1570
sales@pickdiversity.com

PICKDiversity Program Magazine

PICKDiversity
PO Box 696
Solvang, CA 93464
PH: (805) 688-2488
FAX: (805) 686-1570
www.pickdiversity.com
info@pickdiversity.com

TYPE/ FREQUENCY: Magazine/ Quarterly

DESCRIPTION:
Official magazine of the PICKDiversity career fairs.

COVERAGE: USA

RATES:
1/4 page $250; full page $900.

RECRUITING SECTION: Professionals

AUDIENCE CHARACTERISTICS:
• College Graduates

ADVERTISING CONTACT:
Sales Department
PH: (805) 688-2488
FAX: (805) 686-1570
sales@pickdiversity.com

PICKDiversity.com

PICKDiversity
PO Box 696
Solvang, CA 93464
PH: (805) 688-2488
FAX: (805) 686-1570
www.pickdiversity.com
info@pickdiversity.com

TYPE/ FREQUENCY: Web site/ Daily

DESCRIPTION:
Job search web site directed at diverse audience.

COVERAGE: Global

RATES:
6-month web site membership $1,200; 1 year $2,500.

RECRUITING SECTION: Professionals

AUDIENCE CHARACTERISTICS:
• College Graduates

ADVERTISING CONTACT:
Sales Department
PH: (805) 688-2488
FAX: (805) 686-1570
sales@pickdiversity.com

Project Earn

3 Skyline Pl., #600
5201 Leesburg Pike
Falls Church, VA 22041
PH: (866) 327-6669
FAX: (703) 820-4820
www.earnworks.com
projectearn@birchdavis.com

TYPE/ FREQUENCY: Resource center/ Daily

DESCRIPTION:
Federally funded project that connects employers with local rehabilitation, job training, and job placement services for persons with disabilities.

COVERAGE: USA

RATES:
Free.

RECRUITING SECTION: General Recruitment

AUDIENCE CHARACTERISTICS:
• Trade/Professional School Graduates, High School Graduates, College Graduates

ADVERTISING CONTACT:
Customer Service
PH: (866) 327-6669
FAX: (703) 820-4820
projectearn@birchdavis.com

The Providence American

The Amerzine Company
131 Washington St., #212
Providence, RI 02903
PH: (401) 351-8860
FAX: (401) 351-8865

TYPE/ FREQUENCY: Newspaper/ Weekly

DESCRIPTION:
Serving the needs of the minority community in Rhode Island and Southeastern Massachusetts.

CIRCULATION/ AUDITED BY: 5,000/ CPVS

COVERAGE: RI, MA

RATES:
Classifieds: $9 per line or $16 per column inch.

RECRUITING SECTION: General Recruitment

AUDIENCE CHARACTERISTICS:
• High School Graduates, College Graduates

ADVERTISING CONTACT:
Advertising
PH: (401) 351-8860
FAX: (401) 351-8865
amerzine@ix.netcom.com; providenceamerican@hotmail.com

recruitABILITY

DisabledPerson.com
PO Box 230636
Encinitas, CA 92023-0636
PH: (619) 988-8817
FAX: (760) 753-2954
www.disabledperson.com
disabledperson@aol.com

TYPE/ FREQUENCY: Web site/ Daily

DESCRIPTION:
Recruiting source that is part of an online community for persons with disabilities.

COVERAGE: Global

RATES:
$95 per job post (2-month listing).

RECRUITING SECTION: General Recruitment

AUDIENCE CHARACTERISTICS:
• College Graduates

ADVERTISING CONTACT:
PH: (619) 988-8817
FAX: (760) 753-2954
disabledperson@aol.com

Review of Black Political Economy

Transaction Publishers
Rutgers University
New Brunswick, NJ 08903
PH: (732) 445-2280
FAX: (732) 445-3138
www.transactionpublishers.com
trans@transactionpublishers.com

TYPE/ FREQUENCY: Journal/ Quarterly

DESCRIPTION:
A publication of the National Economic Association, it examines issues related to the economic status of African American and Third World peoples.

CIRCULATION/ AUDITED BY: 800

COVERAGE: USA

RATES:
$400 full page.

RECRUITING SECTION: Professionals

AUDIENCE CHARACTERISTICS:
- College Graduates
- Higher Education

ADVERTISING CONTACT:
Advertising
PH: (732) 445-2280
FAX: (732) 445-3138
trans@transactionpublishers.com

Rialto Record

Inland Empire Community Newspapers
PO Box 6247
San Bernardino, CA 92412
PH: (909) 381-9898
FAX: (909) 384-0406

TYPE/ FREQUENCY: Newspaper/ Weekly

DESCRIPTION:
Community newspaper that reaches a largely Hispanic audience.

CIRCULATION/ AUDITED BY: 98,000

COVERAGE: San Bernadino, CA

RATES:
$16.90 per column inch.

RECRUITING SECTION: General Recruitment

AUDIENCE CHARACTERISTICS:
- Spanish Language

ADVERTISING CONTACT:
Kathy Boswell
Classifieds
PH: (909) 381-9898
FAX: (909) 384-0406

SACNAS Conference Program

Society for the Advancement of Chicanos and Native Americans in Science
PO Box 8526
Albuquerque, NM 95060-8526
PH: (831) 459-0170
FAX: (831) 459-0194
www.sacnas.org
info@sacnas.org

TYPE/ FREQUENCY: Conference Program/ Annually

DESCRIPTION:
SACNAS's official National Conference Program allows advertisers to reach over 2,000 science students, faculty, professionals, and K-12 educators.

CIRCULATION/ AUDITED BY: 2,000

COVERAGE: USA

RATES:
1/4 page b/w $500; 1/2 page $1,000; full-page color $3,000.

RECRUITING SECTION: Advanced Technologies

AUDIENCE CHARACTERISTICS:
- Computers/Information Technology, Sciences, Engineering

ADVERTISING CONTACT:
Jean-Paul Cane
PH: (831) 459-0170 ext. 236
FAX: (831) 459-0194
webads@sacnas.org

SACNAS.com

Society for the Advancement of Chicanos and Native Americans in Science
PO Box 8526
Santa Cruz, CA 90561-8526
PH: (831) 459-0170
FAX: (831) 459-0194
www.sacnas.org
info@sacnas.org

TYPE/ FREQUENCY: Web site/ Daily

DESCRIPTION:
The mission of SACNAS is to encourage Chicano/Latino and Native American students to pursue graduate education and obtain the advanced degrees necessary for research careers and science teaching professions at all levels.

COVERAGE: Global

RATES:
$250 per month for text ad with links; 500 word maximum.

RECRUITING SECTION: Advanced Technologies

AUDIENCE CHARACTERISTICS:
- Postgraduate Degree Holders
- Sciences
- Spanish Language

ADVERTISING CONTACT:
Jean-Paul Cane
PH: (831) 459-0170 x236
FAX: (831) 459-0194
webads@sacnas.org

Sacramento Observer

2330 Alhambra Blvd.
Sacramento, CA 95817
PH: (916) 452-4781
www.sacobserver.com
info@sacobserver.com

TYPE/ FREQUENCY: Newspaper/ Weekly

DESCRIPTION:
African American community newspaper.

CIRCULATION/ AUDITED BY: 49,600/ CPVS

COVERAGE: Sacramento, CA

RATES:
$30 per column inch with a minimum of 3 inches.

RECRUITING SECTION: General Recruitment

AUDIENCE CHARACTERISTICS:
• High School Graduates, College Graduates

ADVERTISING CONTACT:
Classifieds
PH: (916) 452-4781
FAX: (916) 452-7744
advertise@sacobserver.com

Saludos.com

Saludos Hispanos
73-121 Fred Waring Dr., #100
Palm Desert, CA 92260
PH: (800) 371-4456
FAX: (760) 776-1214
www.saludos.com
info@saludos.com

TYPE/ FREQUENCY: Web site/ Daily

DESCRIPTION:
Hispanic employment service for jobs, workforce diversity.

COVERAGE: Global

RATES:
$99 per job posting per month; packages available.

RECRUITING SECTION: General Recruitment

AUDIENCE CHARACTERISTICS:
• College Graduates
• Spanish Language

ADVERTISING CONTACT:
Sales
PH: (760) 776-1206
FAX: (760) 766-1214
info@saludos.com

San Francisco Bay View

4908 3rd St.
San Francisco, CA 94124
PH: (415) 671-0449
FAX: (415) 882-8971
www.sfbayview.com
editor@sfbayview.com

TYPE/ FREQUENCY: Newspaper/ Weekly

DESCRIPTION:
Established in 1976 is a free weekly newspaper dedicated to the enlightenment and empowerment of the African American community.

CIRCULATION/ AUDITED BY: 20,000

COVERAGE: San Francisco, CA

RATES:
Local rate: $15 per column inch; national rate: $18 per column inch.

RECRUITING SECTION: General Recruitment

AUDIENCE CHARACTERISTICS:
• College Graduates

ADVERTISING CONTACT:
Classifieds
PH: (415) 671-0449
FAX: (415) 882-8971
editor@sfbayview.com

SCEA.org

Silicon Valley Chinese Engineer Association
PO Box 612283
San Jose, CA 95161-2283
PH: (408) 671-0011
www.scea.org
sponsor@scea.org

TYPE/ FREQUENCY: Web site/ Daily

DESCRIPTION:
SCEA represents a large talent pool of highly educated and highly specialized entrepreneurial Chinese high-tech professionals.

COVERAGE: Global

RATES:
Sponsorship: Platinum $2500 per year (entitles company to free job listings for a year on web site as well as links and participation at SCEA events).

RECRUITING SECTION: Advanced Technologies

AUDIENCE CHARACTERISTICS:
• College Graduates
• High-Tech
• Computers/Information Technology
• Chinese Language

ADVERTISING CONTACT:
Sponsorship
PH: (408) 671-0011
sponsor@scea.org

SeniorJobBank.org

Senior Job Bank, Inc.
PO Box 955
Macclenny, FL 32063
PH: (904) 259-7081
www.seniorjobbank.org
founder@seniorjobbank.org

TYPE/ FREQUENCY: Web site/ Daily

DESCRIPTION:
A nonprofit referral service connecting seniors with part-time, temporary, occasional, and full-time work.

COVERAGE: Global

RATES:
Free.

RECRUITING SECTION: General Recruitment

AUDIENCE CHARACTERISTICS:
• High School Graduates, College Graduates

ADVERTISING CONTACT:
Job Postings
PH: (904) 259-7081
founder@seniorjobbank.org

SeniorTechs.com

The Senior Staff Job Information Database
PO Box 1382
Campbell, CA 95009-1382
PH: (408) 371-9064
FAX: (408) 371-3255
www.seniortech.com
info@seniortechs.com

TYPE/ FREQUENCY: Web site/ Daily

DESCRIPTION:
Connects companies with experienced workers through extensive database of people with extensive expertise in tech fields. NOT an employment agency.

COVERAGE: Global

RATES:
$500 retainer fee for 1 year access to the database; retainer applies to first hire; hire fee of $1,000.

RECRUITING SECTION: Advanced Technologies

AUDIENCE CHARACTERISTICS:
• College Graduates
• High-Tech
• Advanced Technologies

ADVERTISING CONTACT:
Bill Payson
PH: (408) 371-9064
FAX: (408) 371-3255
info@seniortechs.com

Ser Career Fairs

Ser National Jobs for Progress, Inc.
100 Decker Dr., #200
Irving, TX 75062
PH: (972) 541-0616
FAX: (972) 650-0842
www.sernational.org

TYPE/ FREQUENCY: Career fair

DESCRIPTION:
National headquarters of organization promoting the employment of Hispanics around the country.

COVERAGE: USA

RATES:
Call for events and rates.

RECRUITING SECTION: General Recruitment

AUDIENCE CHARACTERISTICS:
• Spanish Language

ADVERTISING CONTACT:
Career Fairs
PH: (972) 541-0616
FAX: (972) 650-0842

Sernational.org

Ser National Jobs for Progress, Inc.
100 Decker Dr.
#200
Irving, TX 75062
PH: (972) 541-0616
FAX: (972) 650-0842
www.sernational.org

TYPE/ FREQUENCY: Web site/ Daily

DESCRIPTION:
National headquarters of organization promoting the employment of Hispanics around the country.

COVERAGE: Global

RATES:
$100 per job per month; other packages available.

RECRUITING SECTION: General Recruitment

AUDIENCE CHARACTERISTICS:
• Spanish Language

ADVERTISING CONTACT:
HeadHunter.net
PH: (877) 235-8978

SHPE Annual Convention

Society of Hispanic Professional Engineers
5400 E. Olympic Blvd., #210
Los Angeles, CA 90022
PH: (323) 725-3970
FAX: (323) 725-0316
www.shpe.org
shpenational@shpe.org

TYPE/ FREQUENCY: Conference/ Annually

DESCRIPTION:
A national not-for-profit organization that promotes Hispanics in engineering, math, and science. Annual convention.

COVERAGE: USA

RATES:
Contact for rates.

RECRUITING SECTION: Advanced Technologies

AUDIENCE CHARACTERISTICS:
• College Graduates
• High-Tech
• Engineering, Sciences
• Spanish Language

ADVERTISING CONTACT:
Convention
PH: (323) 725-3970
FAX: (323) 725-0316
shpenational@shpe.org

SHPE Magazine

Society of Hispanic Professional Engineers
5400 E. Olympic Blvd., #210
Los Angeles, CA 90022
PH: (323) 725-3970
FAX: (323) 725-0316
www.shpe.org
shpenational@shpe.org

TYPE/ FREQUENCY: Magazine/ Quarterly

DESCRIPTION:
A national not-for profit organization that promotes Hispanics in engineering, math, and science. Official magazine.

CIRCULATION/ AUDITED BY: 6,800

COVERAGE: USA

RATES:
1/4 page b/w $1765; 1/2 page b/w $2,845 (prices for single insertion).

RECRUITING SECTION: Advanced Technologies

AUDIENCE CHARACTERISTICS:
• College Graduates
• High-Tech
• Engineering, Sciences
• Spanish Language

ADVERTISING CONTACT:
John Good rich
PH: (770) 442-3290
john.goodrich@shpe.org

SHPE.org

Society of Hispanic Professional Engineers
5400 E. Olympic Blvd., #210
Los Angeles, CA 90022
PH: (323) 725-3970
FAX: (323) 725-0316
www.shpe.org
shpenational@shpe.org

TYPE/ FREQUENCY: Web site/ Daily

DESCRIPTION:
A national not-for-profit organization that promotes Hispanics in engineering, math, and science. Career services portion of web site powered by Brass Ring.

COVERAGE: Global

RATES:
$100 per job posting; packages are available.

RECRUITING SECTION: Advanced Technologies

AUDIENCE CHARACTERISTICS:
- College Graduates
- High-Tech
- Engineering, Sciences
- Spanish Language

ADVERTISING CONTACT:
John Goodrich
PH: (770) 442-3290
john.goodrich@shpe.org

Sing Tao Newspaper

Sing Tao Newspapers New York Ltd.
188 Lafayette St.
New York, NY 10013
PH: (212) 699-3800
FAX: (212) 699-3833

TYPE/ FREQUENCY: Newspaper/ Daily

DESCRIPTION:
Community newspaper targeted to the Chinese American community in the metro area.

CIRCULATION/ AUDITED BY: 55,000

COVERAGE: New York, NY

RATES:
$30 for minimum of 3 consecutive days; $55 weekly.

RECRUITING SECTION: General Recruitment

AUDIENCE CHARACTERISTICS:
- Chinese Language

ADVERTISING CONTACT:
Classifieds
PH: (212) 699-3800
FAX: (212) 699-3833

The Skanner

The Skanner News Group
PO Box 5455
Portland, OR 97228
PH: (503) 285-5555
www.theskanner.com
info@theskanner.com

TYPE/ FREQUENCY: Newspaper/ Weekly

DESCRIPTION:
A weekly newspaper published in Portland, OR, and Seattle, WA, advancing the cause of the Black press in that area.

CIRCULATION/ AUDITED BY: 75,000

COVERAGE: Portland, OR; Seattle, WA

RATES:
Open classified rate: $14.50 per column inch.

RECRUITING SECTION: General Recruitment

AUDIENCE CHARACTERISTICS:
- High School Graduates, College Graduates

ADVERTISING CONTACT:
Classifieds
PH: (503) 285-5555
infor@theskanner.com

South Suburban Standard

Standard Newspapers
615 S. Halsted
Chicago Heights, IL 60411
PH: (312) 755-5021
www.standardnewspapers.com

TYPE/ FREQUENCY: Newspaper/ Weekly

DESCRIPTION:
African American community news.

CIRCULATION/ AUDITED BY: 25,000

COVERAGE: South Suburbs, Chicago IL

RATES:
Contact for rates.

RECRUITING SECTION: General Recruitment

AUDIENCE CHARACTERISTICS:
- High School Graduates, College Graduates

ADVERTISING CONTACT:
PH: (312) 755-5021

Southwest Digest Newspaper

Southwest Digest
902 E. 28th St.
Lubbock, TX 79404
PH: (806) 762-3612
FAX: (806) 745-6675

TYPE/ FREQUENCY: Newspaper/ Weekly

DESCRIPTION:
Southwest Digest has been published every year for 17 years and is designed to help your business reach the 50,000 African Americans living in Lubbock and the entire West Texas and Eastern New Mexico area.

CIRCULATION/ AUDITED BY: 20,000/ CPVS

COVERAGE: West TX, Eastern NM

RATES:
Classifieds: 20 word minimum, 50¢ per word.

RECRUITING SECTION: General Recruitment

AUDIENCE CHARACTERISTICS:
• High School Graduates, College Graduates

ADVERTISING CONTACT:
Eddie Richardson
PH: (806) 745-9292
FAX: (806) 745-6675

Speakin' Out News

115 Wholesale Ave.
PO Box 2826
Huntsville, AL 35804
PH: (256) 551-1020
FAX: (256) 551-0607
www.speakinoutnews.com

TYPE/ FREQUENCY: Newspaper/ Weekly

DESCRIPTION:
Over 21 years' experience offering a viable perspective of African American affairs.

CIRCULATION/ AUDITED BY: 26,000

COVERAGE: Huntsville, Decatur AL; Tennessee Valley

RATES:
Local rate: $10 per column inch; national rate: $18.65 per column inch.

RECRUITING SECTION: General Recruitment

AUDIENCE CHARACTERISTICS:
• College Graduates

ADVERTISING CONTACT:
Advertising
PH: (256) 551-1020
FAX: (256) 551-0607
wsmoth193@aol.com

The Spokesman-Recorder

3744 4th Ave. S
Minneapolis, MN 55409
PH: (612) 827-4021
FAX: (612) 827-0577
www.spokesman-recorder.com

TYPE/ FREQUENCY: Newspaper/ Weekly

DESCRIPTION:
African American community news.

CIRCULATION/ AUDITED BY: 26,000

COVERAGE: Minneapolis, MN

RATES:
$31.49 per column inch.

RECRUITING SECTION: General Recruitment

AUDIENCE CHARACTERISTICS:
• High School Graduates, College Graduates

ADVERTISING CONTACT:
Classifieds
PH: (612) 827-4021
FAX: (612) 827-0577
classifieds@spokesman-recorder.com

St. Louis American

4242 Lindell Blvd.
St. Louis, MO 63108
PH: (314) 533-8000
FAX: (314) 533-2332
www.stlamerican.com

TYPE/ FREQUENCY: Newspaper/ Weekly

DESCRIPTION:
Missouri's most widely read weekly newspaper targeted to African Americans.

CIRCULATION/ AUDITED BY: 65,000/ CAC

COVERAGE: St. Louis, MO

RATES:
$17.25 per column inch.

RECRUITING SECTION: General Recruitment

AUDIENCE CHARACTERISTICS:
• College Graduates

ADVERTISING CONTACT:
Shelitha Peppers
Sales Assistant
PH: (314) 289-5425
FAX: (314) 533-2332
speppers@stlamerican.com

St. Louis Chinese American News

8601 Olive Blvd.
Jeffrey Plaza
St. Louis, MO 63132
PH: (314) 432-3858
FAX: (314) 432-1217
www.scanews.com
sales@scanews.com

TYPE/ FREQUENCY: Newspaper/ Weekly

DESCRIPTION:
Asian American community newspaper.

CIRCULATION/ AUDITED BY: 5,000

COVERAGE: St. Louis, MO

RATES:
$10 per 20 words.

RECRUITING SECTION: General Recruitment

AUDIENCE CHARACTERISTICS:
• Chinese Language

ADVERTISING CONTACT:
Advertising
PH: (314) 432-3858
FAX: (314) 432-3858
sales@scanews.com

St. Louis Sentinel

The St. Louis Sentinel Newspaper
2900 N. Market
St. Louis, MO 63106
PH: (314) 531-2101
FAX: (314) 531-4442
www.stlsentinel.com
stlsenws@swbell.net

TYPE/ FREQUENCY: Newspaper/ Weekly

DESCRIPTION:
The Black political voice of the city.

CIRCULATION/ AUDITED BY: 100,000

COVERAGE: St. Louis, MO

RATES:
Contact for rates.

RECRUITING SECTION: General Recruitment

ADVERTISING CONTACT:
Classifieds
PH: (314) 531-2101
FAX: (314) 531-4442
stlsenws@swbell.com

Sun Reporter

Sun Publishing Company
1791 Bancroft Ave.
San Francisco, CA 94111
PH: (415) 671-1000
FAX: (415) 671-1005
www.sunreporter.com
sundoc97@aol.com

TYPE/ FREQUENCY: Newspaper/ Weekly

DESCRIPTION:
Northern California's oldest, largest, and most influential Black press.

CIRCULATION/ AUDITED BY: 11,000

COVERAGE: Northern CA

RATES:
$15 per 20 words.

RECRUITING SECTION: General Recruitment

ADVERTISING CONTACT:
PH: (415) 671-1000
FAX: (415) 671-1005
sundoc97@aol.com

SVCwireless.org

Silicon Valley Chinese Wireless Technology Association
PO Box 360184
Milpitas, CA 95036-0184
PH: (408) 420-6842
www.svcwireless.org
svcwireless-sponsorship@yahoogroups.com

TYPE/ FREQUENCY: E-mail list/ Daily

DESCRIPTION:
SVC Wireless serves the interests of Chinese professionals in the wireless industry in Silicon Valley. Sponsors can post jobs to mailing list.

COVERAGE: CA

RATES:
Platinum sponsor: $2,000 per year, unlimited job postings; Gold: $1,000 per year, unlimited job postings; Silver: $500 per year up to 10 postings per year.

RECRUITING SECTION: Advanced Technologies

AUDIENCE CHARACTERISTICS:
- College Graduates
- High-Tech
- Computers/Information Technology
- Chinese Language

ADVERTISING CONTACT:
Pearl Tang
VP of Corporate Sponsorships
svcwireless-sponsorship@yahoogroups.com

SWE Annual Convention

Society of Women Engineers
230 E. Ohio St., #400
Chicago, IL 60611
PH: (312) 596-5223
FAX: (312) 644-8557
www.swe.org
hq@swe.org

TYPE/ FREQUENCY: Conference/ Annually

DESCRIPTION:
SWE is an educational organization supporting women in the engineering fields. Annual convention has a career fair and sponsorship opportunities.

COVERAGE: USA

RATES:
Contact for rates.

RECRUITING SECTION: Advanced Technologies

AUDIENCE CHARACTERISTICS:
- College Graduates
- High-Tech
- Engineering, Sciences

ADVERTISING CONTACT:
SWE Conference Management
PH: (800) 892-2858
FAX: (630) 271-8234

SWE Magazine

Society of Women Engineers
230 E. Ohio St., #400
Chicago, IL 60611
PH: (312) 596-5223
FAX: (312) 644-8557
www.swe.org
hq@swe.org

TYPE/ FREQUENCY: Magazine/ Bimonthly

DESCRIPTION:
SWE is an educational organization supporting women in the engineering fields. Official magazine of organization.

COVERAGE: USA

RATES:
1/4 page b/w $1695; 1/2 page b/w $2,795 .

RECRUITING SECTION: Advanced Technologies

AUDIENCE CHARACTERISTICS:
- College Graduates
- High-Tech
- Engineering, Sciences

ADVERTISING CONTACT:
John Goodrich
PH: (770) 442-3290
john.goodrich@swe.org

SWE.org

Society of Women Engineers
230 E. Ohio St., #400
Chicago, IL 60611
PH: (312) 596-5223
FAX: (312) 644-8557
www.swe.org
hq@swe.org

TYPE/ FREQUENCY: Web site/ Daily

DESCRIPTION:
SWE is an educational organization supporting women in the engineering fields. Career job match portion of web site is powered by Brass Ring.

COVERAGE: Global

RECRUITING TOOLS

RATES:
$100 per job posting; packages are available.

RECRUITING SECTION: Advanced Technologies

AUDIENCE CHARACTERISTICS:
• College Graduates
• High-Tech
• Engineering, Sciences

ADVERTISING CONTACT:
John Goodrich
PH: (770) 442-3290
john.goodrich@swe.org

TAOnline.com

Transition Assistance Online
3384 Peachtree Rd., #700
Atlanta, GA 30326
PH: (888) 213-8587
FAX: (404) 239-5690
www.taonline.com
sales@taonline.com

TYPE/ FREQUENCY: Web site/ Daily

DESCRIPTION:
Jobs for transitioning servicemembers and veterans.

CIRCULATION/ AUDITED BY: 1,000,000 per month

COVERAGE: Global

RATES:
Single job posting for 30 days: $100, for 3 months: $250; up to 15 postings: $500, for 3 months: $1,250; unlimited job postings: $750, for 3 months: $2,250; resume search: unlimited, for 30 days: $300, for 60 days: $500, for 1 year: $2,000.

RECRUITING SECTION: General Recruitment

AUDIENCE CHARACTERISTICS:
• High School Graduates, College Graduates

ADVERTISING CONTACT:
Chris Gillette
Director of Sales
PH: (888) 213-8587
FAX: (404) 239-5690
cgillette@taonline.com

TBWCareers.com

The Black World Today
PO Box 328
Randallstown, MD 21133
PH: (410) 521-4678
FAX: (410) 521-9993
www.tbwt.com

TYPE/ FREQUENCY: Web site/ Daily

DESCRIPTION:
TBWT publishes high-quality content on the web career page and is powered by Career Engine.

COVERAGE: Global

RATES:
$175 per job.

RECRUITING SECTION: Professionals

ADVERTISING CONTACT:
TBWT/Career Engine
PH: (877) Job FOCUS
info@careerengine.com

Tennessee Tribune

1501 Jefferson St.
Nashville, TN 37208
PH: (615) 321-9551
FAX: (615) 321-0409
www.tennessetribune.com

TYPE/ FREQUENCY: Newspaper/ Weekly

DESCRIPTION:
African American community newspaper with a largely affluent and professional audience.

CIRCULATION/ AUDITED BY: 45,000

COVERAGE: Nashville, TN

RATES:
$22 per column inch display rate; classified rate: $4.50 for 3-6 lines, $7.00 for 7-10 lines.

RECRUITING SECTION: Professionals

ADVERTISING CONTACT:
Bill Thompson
Advertising
PH: (615)321-9551
FAX: (615) 321-0409

Title VII Diversity Career Fair Exhibitor Guide

Career Fair Productions
13101 Washington Blvd., #141
Los Angeles, CA 90066
PH: (310) 566-7474
FAX: (310) 566-7471
www.careerfairproductions.com
info@careerfairproductions.com

TYPE/ FREQUENCY: Exhibitor's Guide/ Bimonthly

DESCRIPTION:
Exhibitors' guide for Title VII career fairs.

COVERAGE: USA

RATES:
1/2 page $600; full page $800.

RECRUITING SECTION: General Recruitment

AUDIENCE CHARACTERISTICS:
• College Graduates

ADVERTISING CONTACT:
Title VII Career Fairs
PH: (310) 566-7474

Title VII Diversity Career Fairs

Career Fair Productions
13101 Washington Blvd., #141
Los Angeles, CA 90066
PH: (310) 566-7474
FAX: (310) 566-7471
www.careerfairproductions.com
info@careerfairproductions.com

TYPE/ FREQUENCY: Career fair/ Bimonthly

DESCRIPTION:
Career Fair provides recruiters access to the United States' largest pool of diverse, multicultural, and qualified professionals.

COVERAGE: USA

RATES:
$2,695 per booth as advance discount rate; standard rates higher.

RECRUITING SECTION: General Recruitment

AUDIENCE CHARACTERISTICS:
• College Graduates

ADVERTISING CONTACT:
Title VII Career Fairs
PH: (310) 566-7474

Transition Bulletin Board

Operation Transition
Department of Defense
Washington, DC 20301
PH: (703) 697-5737
www.dmdc.osd.mil
dorshelp@osd.pentagon.mil

TYPE/ FREQUENCY: Web site/ Daily

DESCRIPTION:
Operation Transition was designed to link employers with highly qualified job seekers. TBB is a database of job want ads and other career information established to help separating DOD personnel transition back into civilian life.

CIRCULATION/ AUDITED BY: 30,000

COVERAGE: Global

RATES:
Free; must register.

RECRUITING SECTION: General Recruitment

AUDIENCE CHARACTERISTICS:
• High School Graduates, College Graduates

ADVERTISING CONTACT:
Help Desk
dorshelp@osd.pentagon.mil

Tri-State Defender

124 E. Calhoun Ave.
Memphis, TN 38103
PH: (901) 523-1814
FAX: (901) 523-1820

TYPE/ FREQUENCY: Newspaper/ Weekly

DESCRIPTION:
African American community news.

COVERAGE: Memphis, TN

RATES:
$1.05 per line or $14.70 per column inch.

RECRUITING SECTION: General Recruitment

AUDIENCE CHARACTERISTICS:
• High School Graduates, College Graduates

ADVERTISING CONTACT:
Myron Hudson
Classified Sales Manager
PH: (901) 523-1814
FAX: (901) 523-1820

Twin Visions

221 Washington St.
2nd Floor
Newark, NJ 07102
PH: (973) 642-2888
FAX: (973) 642-2850
www.twinvisionsweekly.com
twinsuccess@aol.com

TYPE/ FREQUENCY: Newspaper/ Weekly

DESCRIPTION:
African American community news.

CIRCULATION/ AUDITED BY: 30,000

COVERAGE: Newark, NJ

RATES:
20 words $17.60; 30 words $22; 40 words $26.40; 50 words $30.80; 60 words $35.20.

RECRUITING SECTION: General Recruitment

AUDIENCE CHARACTERISTICS:
• High School Graduates, College Graduates

ADVERTISING CONTACT:
Classifieds
PH: (973) 642-2888
FAX: (973) 642-2850
twinsuccess@aol.com

The Urban Spectrum

PO Box 31001
Aurora, CO 80041
PH: (303) 292-6446
FAX: (303) 292-6543
urbanspectrum@qwest.com

TYPE/ FREQUENCY: Newspaper/ Monthly

DESCRIPTION:
The Urban Spectrum is a free, monthly publication dedicated to Denver's multicultural interests.

CIRCULATION/ AUDITED BY: 60,000

COVERAGE: Denver, CO

RATES:
Classified rates: $34 per column inch.

RECRUITING SECTION: General Recruitment

AUDIENCE CHARACTERISTICS:
• College Graduates

ADVERTISING CONTACT:
Classifieds
PH: (303) 292-6446
FAX: (303) 292-6543
urbanspectrum@qwest.net

Veteran's Enterprise

E. M. Publishing Enterprises
19456 Ventura Blvd., #200
Tarzana, CA 91356
PH: (818) 774-0870
FAX: (818) 654-0874
empei@aol.com

TYPE/ FREQUENCY: Magazine/ Quarterly

DESCRIPTION:
The military and veteran's business network.

CIRCULATION/ AUDITED BY: 7,500/ BPA

COVERAGE: USA

RATES:
Contact for rates.

RECRUITING SECTION: Professionals

AUDIENCE CHARACTERISTICS:
• College Graduates

ADVERTISING CONTACT:
Dariush Pasha
Sales Manager
PH: (818) 774-1931
FAX: (818) 654-0874

Veteran's Vision

E. M. Publishing Enterprises
19456 Ventura Blvd., #200
Tarzana, CA 91356
PH: (818) 774-0870
FAX: (818) 654-0874
empei@aol.com

TYPE/ FREQUENCY: Magazine/ Quarterly

DESCRIPTION:
The official publication of Brotherhood Rally of all veterans' organizations.

CIRCULATION/ AUDITED BY: 7,500

COVERAGE: USA

RATES:
Contact for rates.

RECRUITING SECTION: Professionals

AUDIENCE CHARACTERISTICS:
• College Graduates

ADVERTISING CONTACT:
Dariush Pasha
Sales Manager
PH: (818) 774-1931
FAX: (818) 654-0874

VetJobs.com

PO Box 71445
Marietta, GA 30007-1445
PH: (770) 993-5117
FAX: (770) 993-2875
www.vetjobs.com
info@vetjobs.com

TYPE/ FREQUENCY: Web site/ Daily

DESCRIPTION:
A web site for all former military personnel both transitioning and those that are already in the civilian workforce. It is free for vets.

COVERAGE: Global

RATES:
Single job posting: $120 per job; resume membership: $2,400 per year; job posting membership: $4,200 per year; 50 job posts (including resume access): $4,750; full membership: $6,000 per year.

RECRUITING SECTION: General Recruitment

AUDIENCE CHARACTERISTICS:
• High School Graduates, College Graduates

ADVERTISING CONTACT:
Membership
PH: (770) 993-5117
FAX: (770) 993-2875
info@vetjobs.com

The Washington Afro-American

The Afro-American Newspaper Co.
2519 N. Charles St.
Baltimore, MD 21218
PH: (410) 554-8200
FAX: (410) 554-8213

TYPE/ FREQUENCY: Newspaper/ Weekly

DESCRIPTION:
Serving the African American community in Washington, DC.

CIRCULATION/ AUDITED BY: 45,000

COVERAGE: Washington, DC

RATES:
$15.78 per column inch.

RECRUITING SECTION: General Recruitment

AUDIENCE CHARACTERISTICS:
• College Graduates

ADVERTISING CONTACT:
Bill Smith
Classifieds
PH: (410) 554-8200
FAX: (410) 554-8213

The Washington Informer

The Washington Informer Newspaper
3117 Martin Luther King Jr. Ave.
Washington, DC 20032
PH: (202) 561-4100
FAX: (202) 574-3785
washington.informer@verizon.net

TYPE/ FREQUENCY: Newspaper/ Weekly

DESCRIPTION:
African American community newspaper.

CIRCULATION/ AUDITED BY: 27,000/ CPVS

COVERAGE: Washington, DC

RATES:
Local rate: $15 per column inch; national: $18 per column inch.

RECRUITING SECTION: Professionals

AUDIENCE CHARACTERISTICS:
• College Graduates

ADVERTISING CONTACT:
Classifieds
PH: (202) 561-4100
FAX: (202) 574-3785
washington.informer@verizon.net

WITI4Hire

Women in Technology
6345 Balboa Blvd., #257
Encino, CA 91316
PH: (800) 334-WITI
FAX: (818) 342-9891
www.witi.com
info@corp.witi.com

TYPE/ FREQUENCY: Web site/ Daily

DESCRIPTION:
Women in Technology International's official job site.

COVERAGE: Global

RATES:
$100 per job posting; packages are available.

RECRUITING SECTION: Advanced Technologies

AUDIENCE CHARACTERISTICS:
• College Graduates
• High-Tech
• Computer/ Information Technology, Engineering

ADVERTISING CONTACT:
Cynthia Roe
Sales
PH: (925) 552-7377
cynthia@corp.witi.com

Woman Engineer

Equal Opportunity Publications, Inc.
445 Broad Hollow Rd., #425
Melville, NY 11747
PH: (631) 421-9421
FAX: (631) 421-0359
www.eop.com
info@eop.com

TYPE/ FREQUENCY: Magazine/ Web site/ Three times per year

DESCRIPTION:
A free magazine offered to women engineering, computer-science, and IT students and professionals seeking to find employment and advance their careers.

CIRCULATION/ AUDITED BY: 14,126/ BPA

COVERAGE: International

RATES:
$250 per month per magazine for online editions; call for print rates.

RECRUITING SECTION: Advanced Technologies

AUDIENCE CHARACTERISTICS:
• College Graduates
• High-Tech
• Engineering

ADVERTISING CONTACT:
Advertising
PH: (631) 421-9421
FAX: (631) 421-0359
info@eop.com

Womcom.org

Association for Women in Communications
780 Ritchie Hwy.
#28-S
Severna Park, MD 21146
PH: (410) 544-7442
FAX: (410) 544-4640
www.womcom.org
pat@womcom.org

TYPE/ FREQUENCY: Web site/ Daily

DESCRIPTION:
Association's job bank is run by Job Options.

COVERAGE: Global

RATES:
$195 per job for 1-9 jobs; posting packages available.

RECRUITING SECTION: Professionals

AUDIENCE CHARACTERISTICS:
• College Graduates
• Communications

ADVERTISING CONTACT:
Job Options
PH: (800) 682-2901
FAX: (216) 566-7388
info@joboptions.com

Women for Hire Career Fairs

Women for Hire
148 W. 72nd St.
2nd Floor
New York, NY 10023
PH: (212) 580-6100
FAX: (212) 579-2400
www.womenforhire.com
info@womenforhire.com

TYPE/ FREQUENCY: Career fair/ Bimonthly

DESCRIPTION:
One-day events that link leading companies with college seniors, graduate students, and professional women with up to 7 years of experience.

COVERAGE: USA

RATES:
Participation in 1-2 events $1,995 per event; 3-4 events $1,795 per event; 5 events $1,595 per event.

RECRUITING SECTION: General Recruitment

AUDIENCE CHARACTERISTICS:
• College Graduates

ADVERTISING CONTACT:
Stephanie Biasi
Sales
PH: (212) 580-6100 ext. 12
FAX: (212) 579-2400
sbiasi@womenforhire.com

Women In Business

American Business Women's Association
9100 Ward Pkwy.
PO Box 8728
Kansas City, MO 64114-0728
PH: (816) 361-6621
FAX: (816) 361-4991
www.abwa.org
wmabrey@abwa.org

TYPE/ FREQUENCY: Magazine/ Bimonthly

DESCRIPTION:
A bimonthly magazine designed to provide information and insight into work-related topics pertinent to women.

CIRCULATION/ AUDITED BY: 70,000

COVERAGE: USA

RATES:
$968 per 1/6 page; $2,182 per 1/2 page.

RECRUITING SECTION: Managers and Executives

AUDIENCE CHARACTERISTICS:
• College Graduates

ADVERTISING CONTACT:
Wendy Mabrey
Corporate Sponsorship
PH: (816) 361-6621 ext. 260
FAX: (816) 361-4991
wmabrey@abwa.org

Women in Natural Resources Web Site

Women in Natural Resources
PO Box 3577
Moscow, ID 83843
PH: (208) 885-6754
FAX: (208) 885-5878
www.ets.uidaho.edu/winr
winr@uidaho.edu

TYPE/ FREQUENCY: Web site/ Daily

DESCRIPTION:
Job web site for WINR.

COVERAGE: Global

RATES:
$140 per job.

RECRUITING SECTION: Professionals

AUDIENCE CHARACTERISTICS:
• College Graduates
• Energy/ Natural Resources
• Sciences

ADVERTISING CONTACT:
Sandra Martin
Editor
PH: (208) 885-6754
FAX: (208) 885-5878
winr@uidaho.edu

Women in Natural Resources Job Flyer

Women in Natural Resources
PO Box 3577
Moscow, ID 83843
PH: (208) 885-6754
FAX: (208) 885-5878
www.ets.uidaho.edu/winr
winr@uidaho.edu

TYPE/ FREQUENCY: Job Listings/ Monthly

DESCRIPTION:
Monthly job flyer.

COVERAGE: USA

RATES:
$550 per 1/2 page; $140 per 1/8 page.

RECRUITING SECTION: Professionals

AUDIENCE CHARACTERISTICS:
• College Graduates
• Energy/ Natural Resources
• Sciences

ADVERTISING CONTACT:
Sandra Martin
Editor
PH: (208) 885-6754
FAX: (208) 885-5878
winr@uidaho.edu

Women in Natural Resources Journal

Women in Natural Resources
PO Box 3577
Moscow, ID 83843
PH: (208) 885-6754
FAX: (208) 885-5878
www.ets.uidaho.edu/winr
winr@uidaho.edu

TYPE/ FREQUENCY: Journal/ Quarterly

DESCRIPTION:
Quarterly journal for women in the field of natural resources.

COVERAGE: USA

RATES:
$550 per 1/2 page; $140 per 1/8 page.

RECRUITING SECTION: Professionals

AUDIENCE CHARACTERISTICS:
• College Graduates
• Energy/ Natural Resources
• Sciences

ADVERTISING CONTACT:
Sandra Martin
Editor
PH: (208) 885-6754
FAX: (208) 885-5878
winr@uidaho.edu

Women Unlimited Job Bank

Women Unlimited
71 Winthrop St.
Augusta, ME 04330
PH: (800) 281-5259
FAX: (207) 623-7299
www.womenunlimited.org

TYPE/ FREQUENCY: Web site/ Daily

DESCRIPTION:
Organization supporting training and employment for women in the construction industry.

CIRCULATION/ AUDITED BY: 800

COVERAGE: ME

RATES:
Free.

RECRUITING SECTION: General Recruitment

AUDIENCE CHARACTERISTICS:
• Construction

ADVERTISING CONTACT:
Job Bank
PH: (207) 623-7576
FAX: (207) 623-7299

Womens Executive Network

516 E. 2nd St.
#13
South Boston, MA 02127
PH: (617) 269-5599
FAX: (617) 269-2697
www.thewen.com
aglynn@thewen.com

TYPE/ FREQUENCY: Web site/ Daily

DESCRIPTION:
Reaches over one million web users per month via a job board co-branded with WorkingWoman.com and NAFE.com.

CIRCULATION/ AUDITED BY: 1,000,000

COVERAGE: Global

RATES:
$150 per job for 45 days; other packages available.

RECRUITING SECTION: Managers and Executives

AUDIENCE CHARACTERISTICS:
• College Graduates

ADVERTISING CONTACT:
A. Glynn
PH: (617) 269-5599
aglynn@thewen.com

The Woo Zone

National Society of Black Engineers
1454 Duke St.
Alexandria, VA 22314
PH: (703) 549-2207
www.nsbe.org
info@nsbe.org

TYPE/ FREQUENCY: Web site/ Daily

DESCRIPTION:
The premier organization linking Black engineers and the African American community to technology and opportunities. Organization's official job site powered by Brass Ring.

COVERAGE: Global

RATES:
$100 per job posting; packages are available.

RECRUITING SECTION: Advanced Technologies

AUDIENCE CHARACTERISTICS:
• College Graduates
• High-Tech
• Engineering, Sciences

ADVERTISING CONTACT:
Brass Ring
PH: (800) 299-7494

Workforce Diversity for Engineering and IT Professionals

Equal Opportunity Publications, Inc.
445 Broad Hollow Rd.
#425
Melville, NY 11747
PH: (631) 421-9421
FAX: (631) 421-0359
www.eop.com
info@eop.com

TYPE/ FREQUENCY: Magazine/ Quarterly

DESCRIPTION:
Free magazine distributed to the diverse high-tech workforce

CIRCULATION/ AUDITED BY: 15,046/ BPA

COVERAGE: USA

RATES:
$250 per month per magazine for online editions; call for print rates.

RECRUITING SECTION: Advanced Technologies

AUDIENCE CHARACTERISTICS:
• College Graduates
• High-Tech
• Computers/Information Technology, Sciences, Engineering

ADVERTISING CONTACT:
Advertising
PH: (631) 421-9421
FAX: (631) 421-0359
info@eop.com

Workforce Recruitment Program for College Students with Disabilities

Office of Disability Employment Policy and Department of Defense
1331 F St. NW
3rd Floor
Washington, DC 20004
PH: (202) 376-6200
FAX: (202) 376-6219
www.wrpjobs.com

TYPE/ FREQUENCY: CD-ROM / Annually

DESCRIPTION:
WRP is a resource for businesses nationwide to identify qualified temporary and permanent employees in a variety of fields. This is a searchable database of more than 1,000 students and recent graduates.

CIRCULATION/ AUDITED BY: 1,000

COVERAGE: USA

RATES:
Free.

RECRUITING SECTION: General Recruitment

AUDIENCE CHARACTERISTICS:
• College Students/Recent Graduates

ADVERTISING CONTACT:
Office of Disability Employment Policy
PH: (202) 376-6200
FAX: (202) 376-6219

WorkplaceDiversity.com

71 S. Orange Ave.
#367
South Orange, NJ 07079
PH: (973) 275-9771
www.workplacediversity.com
info@workplacediversity.com

TYPE/ FREQUENCY: Web site/ Daily

DESCRIPTION:
Is a central job search web site for recruiters who want to make a
good faith effort to expand their recruitment strategies to
promote a diverse workforce.

COVERAGE: Global

RATES:
Single job posting: $175; 10: $1,500; 25: $3,300; 100: $10,500;
250: $21,850. Resume Database access: Monthly: $300; Per Year:
$2,400.

RECRUITING SECTION: Professionals

AUDIENCE CHARACTERISTICS:
• College Graduates

ADVERTISING CONTACT:
Career Engine
PH: (877) Job Focus
info@workplacediversity.com; info@careerengine.com

Lists and Index

RECRUITING TOOLS BY GEOGRAPHICAL COVERAGE

Global Coverage

50andOverboard.com
AABE
AAHCPA.org
AAIP
AAMA
AAUW.org
ABC
Academygrad.com
Advancing Women Network
AdvancingWomen.com
Africareers.com
Afronet.com
AISES.com
Asiancareers.com
ASWA
AWG E-Mail News
AWG Web site
AWIP
AWIS.org
AWM
AWMI
AWP
AWSCPA
BDPA Job Listings
BDPA Journal Online
BIGnet.org
BlackEnterprise.com
BlackStocks.com
BlackVoices.com
Blackworld.com
BlueSuitMom.com
Boston Chapter of NAAAP
Business-Disability.com
Career Opportunity and Exchange
Careers On-Line
Careerwoman2000.com
CareerWomen.com
CASPA
CCNMA
Center on Employment

Cnetwork
Committee on Women in Engineering
Corporate Gray Online
Destinygrp.com
DiversiLink
Diversity Employment
DiversityRecruiting.com
EOP.com
FWA.org
HACE Candidate Referral Service
HACE-USA.ORG
HeadsUp
HireDiversity.com
Hispanicareers.com
HispanicHealth.org
HispanicOnline.com
HNBA.com
Iamable.net
iHispano.com
IMDiversity.com
Inroadsinc.org
iVillage.com
IWITTS.com
JMOJOBS.com
JobAccess.org
LatinoWeb Job Site
LatPro.com
Member Listserv
MilitaryHeadhunter.com
NAAAHR.org
NABA Corporate Career Center
NABJobs
NABTP.org
NAIW.org
NAJA
NAMEPA.org
NAMIC
NAPALSA.org
NAPMW
NASBE.org

NASPHQ.com
NATEA
National Black MBA Job Posting System
NativeAmericanJobs.com
NativeJobs.com
NAWIC Career Center
NBPRS.com
NCOJobs.com
NDNJB
Nemnet
Nemnet
NetNoir.com
NHBA.org
NHCC-HQ.org
NOBCChE.org
NOMA.net
NSBP.org
NSHMBA.org
OpportunityBlvd.com
PICKDiversity.com
recruitABILITY
SACNAS.com
Saludos.com
SCEA.org
SeniorJobBank.org
SeniorTechs.com
Sernational.org
SHPE.org
SWE.org
TAOnline.com
TBWCareers.com
Transition Bulletin Board
VetJobs.com
WITI4Hire
Womcom.org
Women in Natural Resources Web Site
Womens Executive Network
Woo Zone, The
WorkplaceDiversity.com

International Coverage

Hispanic Journal of Behavioral Sciences
Journal of American Ethnic History
Journal of Black Psychology
Journal of Black Studies
Latin American Perspectives
Modern China
Network
Woman Engineer

U.S. Coverage

AAHCPA Career Fair/Expo
AAUW Outlook
ABWA National Convention Career Fair
Affirmative Action Register
African American Career World
American Jewish World
AWIS Magazine
AWRT CareerLine
Black Collegian, The
Black Engineer and Information Technology
Black Enterprise Magazine
Black Issues in Higher Education
Black MBA Magazine
Black MBA Magazine
Black Perspective, The
Black Voices Career Fairs
Bottom Line, The
Brasilian, The
BVQ Magazine
Careers and the Disabled
Careers and the Disabled Career Fair
Challenger Newspaper
Circle News, The
Crisis Magazine, The
Equal Opportunity
FWA News
Gaea
HACE Career Conference
Hire Diversity Career Fairs
Hispanic Business Magazine

Hispanic Career World
Hispanic Engineer and Information
   Technology
Hispanic Link Weekly Report
Hispanic Magazine
Hispanic MBA
Hispanic MBA Career Fairs
Hispanic Nurses Unnamed Journal
Hispanic Today
India Abroad
Indian Country Today
Jewish Business Quarterly
Job Opportunities for the Blind
Journal of African American Men
Journal of the National Black Nurses
   Association
Latino Law Student Job Fair
Minority Engineer
NAACP Career Fairs
NACME Journal
NAHFE Annual Conference
National Association of Hispanic Nurses
   Annual Conference
National Association of Negro Business
   and Professional Womens Clubs Job Line
National Black MBA Career Fairs
National Conference
NAWIC Image
NBNA Conference
NBNA Newsletter

Nemnet
News from Indian Country
NFB Jobline
NSBE Bridge
NSBE Magazine
NSBE National Conference
PICKDiversity Career Fair
PICKDiversity Program Magazine
Project Earn
Review of Black Political Economy
SACNAS Conference Program
Ser Career Fairs
SHPE Annual Convention
SHPE Magazine
SWE Annual Convention
SWE Magazine
Title VII Diversity Career Fair Exhibitor
   Guide
Title VII Diversity Career Fairs
Veteran's Enterprise
Veteran's Vision
Women for Hire Career Fairs
Women In Business
Women in Natural Resources Job Flyer
Women in Natural Resources Journal
Workforce Diversity for Engineering and IT
   Professionals
Workforce Recruitment Program for
   College Students with Disabilities

RECRUITING TOOLS BY GEOGRAPHICAL COVERAGE

U.S. Regional Coverage

FAR WEST

Asian American Times Online
Asian Week
California Advocate, The
Chinese Software Professionals Assoc.
    Annual Conference
Chinese Software Professionals Assoc. Job
    Fair
Colton Courier
CSPA Newsletter
CSPA.com
El Chicano
India-West
Jobs4Women.com
La Oferta
La Opinion
La Prensa San Diego
News from Native California
Nikkei West
NW Asian Weekly
Rialto Record
Sacramento Observer
San Francisco Bay View
Skanner, The
Sun Reporter
SVCwireless.org

MIDWEST

Arab American News, The
Black Chronicle, The
Cherokee Phoenix
Chicago Shimpo, The
Chicago Standard
Chickasaw Times
Denver Indian Center Job Board
Dos Mundos
Hispania News
Indianapolis Recorder
Insight News
La Prensa
Lawndale News Group
Louisville Defender
Miami County Republic
Michigan Chronicle
Milwaukee Times, The
Native American Times
Ojibwe Akiing
Oklahoma Eagle
Omaha Star
South Suburban Standard
Spokesman-Recorder, The
St. Louis American
St. Louis Chinese American News
St. Louis Sentinel
Urban Spectrum, The

NORTHEAST

Amsterdam News
Carib News
Center on Employment
Forward, The
Jewish Chronicle, The
Job Flash Newsletter
New Pittsburgh Courier
Providence American, The
Sing Tao Newspaper
Twin Visions
Washington Informer, The
Women Unlimited Job Bank

SOUTHEAST

Advocate, The
Atlanta Voice, The
Baltimore Afro-American, The
Black News
Charlotte Post
Columbus Times, The
Contempora Magazine
El Heraldo
El Latino
El Popular
el Reportero
Florida Review
Florida Sentinel
La Noticia
Minority Networking Night
Speakin' Out News
Tennessee Tribune
Tri-State Defender
Washington Afro-American, The

SOUTHWEST

Capitol Times, The
Daily Post Tribune
El Sol de Texas
Houston Defender
La Prensa de San Antonio
Southwest Digest Newspaper

Electronic

50andOverboard.com
AABE
AAHCPA.org
AAIP
AAMA
AAUW.org
ABC
Academygrad.com
Advancing Women Network
AdvancingWomen.com
Africareers.com
Afronet.com
AISES.com
Asiancareers.com
ASWA
AWG E-Mail News
AWG Web site
AWIP
AWIS.org
AWM
AWMI
AWP
AWRT CareerLine
AWSCPA
BDPA Job Listings
BDPA Journal Online
BIGnet.org
BlackEnterprise.com
BlackStocks.com
BlackVoices.com
Blackworld.com
BlueSuitMom.com
Boston Chapter of NAAAP
Business-Disability.com
Career Opportunity and Exchange
Careers On-Line
Careerwoman2000.com
CareerWomen.com
CASPA
CCNMA
Center on Employment
Cnetwork
Committee on Women in Engineering
Corporate Gray Online
CSPA.com
Destinygrp.com

DiversiLink
Diversity Employment
DiversityRecruiting.com
EOP.com
FWA.org
HACE Candidate Referral Service
HACE-USA.ORG
HeadsUp
HireDiversity.com
Hispanicareers.com
HispanicHealth.org
HispanicOnline.com
HNBA.com
Iamable.net
iHispano.com
IMDiversity.com
Inroadsinc.org
iVillage.com
IWITTS.com
JMOJOBS.com
JobAccess.org
Jobs4Women.com
LatinoWeb Job Site
LatPro.com
Member Listserv
MilitaryHeadhunter.com
NAAAHR.org
NABA Corporate Career Center
NABJobs
NABTP.org
NAIW.org
NAJA
NAMEPA.org
NAMIC
NAPALSA.org
NAPMW
NASBE.org
NASPHQ.com
NATEA
National Association of Negro Business
   and Professional Womens Clubs Job Line
National Black MBA Job Posting System
NativeAmericanJobs.com
NativeJobs.com
NAWIC Career Center
NBPRS.com

NCOJobs.com
NDNJB
Nemnet
Nemnet
NetNoir.com
NFB Jobline
NHBA.org
NHCC-HQ.org
NOBCChE.org
NOMA.net
NSBP.org
NSHMBA.org
OpportunityBlvd.com
PICKDiversity.com
recruitABILITY
SACNAS.com
Saludos.com
SCEA.org
SeniorJobBank.org
SeniorTechs.com
Sernational.org
SHPE.org
SVCwireless.org
SWE.org
TAOnline.com
TBWCareers.com
Transition Bulletin Board
VetJobs.com
WITI4Hire
Womcom.org
Women in Natural Resources Web Site
Women Unlimited Job Bank
Womens Executive Network
Woo Zone, The
Workforce Recruitment Program for
   College Students with Disabilities
WorkplaceDiversity.com

On-site

AAHCPA Career Fair/Expo
ABWA National Convention Career Fair
Black Voices Career Fairs
Careers and the Disabled Career Fair
Center on Employment
Chinese Software Professionals Assoc.
  Annual Conference
Chinese Software Professionals Assoc. Job
  Fair
Denver Indian Center Job Board
HACE Career Conference

Hire Diversity Career Fairs
Hispanic MBA Career Fairs
Job Opportunities for the Blind
Latino Law Student Job Fair
Minority Networking Night
NAACP Career Fairs
NAHFE Annual Conference
National Association of Hispanic Nurses
  Annual Conference
National Black MBA Career Fairs
National Conference

NBNA Conference
Nemnet
NSBE National Conference
PICKDiversity Career Fair
Project Earn
Ser Career Fairs
SHPE Annual Convention
SWE Annual Convention
Title VII Diversity Career Fairs
Women for Hire Career Fairs

Print

AAUW Outlook
Advocate, The
Affirmative Action Register
African American Career World
American Jewish World
Amsterdam News
Arab American News, The
Asian American Times Online
Asian Week
Atlanta Voice, The
AWIS Magazine
Baltimore Afro-American, The
Black Chronicle, The
Black Collegian, The
Black Engineer and Information Technology
Black Enterprise Magazine
Black Issues in Higher Education
Black MBA Magazine
Black MBA Magazine
Black News
Black Perspective, The
Bottom Line, The
Brasilian, The
BVQ Magazine
California Advocate, The
Capitol Times, The
Careers and the Disabled
Carib News
Challenger Newspaper
Charlotte Post
Cherokee Phoenix
Chicago Shimpo, The
Chicago Standard
Chickasaw Times
Circle News, The
Colton Courier
Columbus Times, The
Contempora Magazine
Crisis Magazine, The
CSPA Newsletter
Daily Post Tribune
Dos Mundos
El Chicano
El Heraldo
El Latino
El Popular
el Reportero
El Sol de Texas
Equal Opportunity

Florida Review
Florida Sentinel
Forward, The
FWA News
Gaea
Hispania News
Hispanic Business Magazine
Hispanic Career World
Hispanic Engineer and Information
   Technology
Hispanic Journal of Behavioral Sciences
Hispanic Link Weekly Report
Hispanic Magazine
Hispanic MBA
Hispanic Nurses Unnamed Journal
Hispanic Today
Houston Defender
India Abroad
Indian Country Today
Indianapolis Recorder
India-West
Insight News
Jewish Business Quarterly
Jewish Chronicle, The
Job Flash Newsletter
Journal of African American Men
Journal of American Ethnic History
Journal of Black Psychology
Journal of Black Studies
Journal of the National Black Nurses
   Association
La Noticia
La Oferta
La Opinion
La Prensa
La Prensa de San Antonio
La Prensa San Diego
Latin American Perspectives
Lawndale News Group
Louisville Defender
Miami County Republic
Michigan Chronicle
Milwaukee Times, The
Minority Engineer
Modern China
NACME Journal
Native American Times
NAWIC Image
NBNA Newsletter

Network
New Pittsburgh Courier
News from Indian Country
News from Native California
Nikkei West
NSBE Bridge
NSBE Magazine
NW Asian Weekly
Ojibwe Akiing
Oklahoma Eagle
Omaha Star
PICKDiversity Program Magazine
Providence American, The
Review of Black Political Economy
Rialto Record
SACNAS Conference Program
Sacramento Observer
San Francisco Bay View
SHPE Magazine
Sing Tao Newspaper
Skanner, The
South Suburban Standard
Southwest Digest Newspaper
Speakin' Out News
Spokesman-Recorder, The
St. Louis American
St. Louis Chinese American News
St. Louis Sentinel
Sun Reporter
SWE Magazine
Tennessee Tribune
Title VII Diversity Career Fair Exhibitor
   Guide
Tri-State Defender
Twin Visions
Urban Spectrum, The
Veteran's Enterprise
Veteran's Vision
Washington Afro-American, The
Washington Informer, The
Woman Engineer
Women In Business
Women in Natural Resources Job Flyer
Women in Natural Resources Journal
Workforce Diversity for Engineering and
   IT Professionals

RECRUITING TOOLS BY LANGUAGE OTHER THAN ENGLISH

Arabic Language

Arab American News, The

Chinese Language

CASPA
Chinese Software Professionals Assoc.
  Annual Conference
Chinese Software Professionals Assoc. Job
  Fair
Cnetwork
CSPA Newsletter
CSPA.com
Modern China
NATEA
SCEA.org
Sing Tao Newspaper
St. Louis Chinese American News
SVCwireless.org

Hindi Language

India Abroad
India-West

Japanese Language

Chicago Shimpo, The
Nikkei West

Portuguese Language

Brasilian, The
Florida Review
LatPro.com

Russian Language

Forward, The

Spanish Language

AAHCPA Career Fair/Expo
AAHCPA.org
Bottom Line, The
Career Opportunity and Exchange
CCNMA
Colton Courier
Dos Mundos
El Chicano
El Heraldo
El Latino
El Popular
el Reportero
El Sol de Texas
HACE Candidate Referral Service
HACE Career Conference
HACE-USA.ORG
Hispania News
Hispanic Business Magazine
Hispanic Career World
Hispanic Engineer and Information
  Technology
Hispanic Journal of Behavioral Sciences
Hispanic Link Weekly Report
Hispanic Magazine
Hispanic MBA
Hispanic Nurses Unnamed Journal
Hispanic Today
Hispanicareers.com
HispanicHealth.org
HispanicOnline.com
HNBA.com
iHispano.com
La Noticia
La Oferta
La Opinion
La Prensa
La Prensa de San Antonio
La Prensa San Diego
Latin American Perspectives
Latino Law Student Job Fair
LatinoWeb Job Site
LatPro.com
Lawndale News Group
NAHFE Annual Conference
National Association of Hispanic Nurses
  Annual Conference
NHBA.org
NHCC-HQ.org
NSHMBA.org
Rialto Record
SACNAS.com
Saludos.com
Ser Career Fairs
Sernational.org
SHPE Annual Convention
SHPE Magazine
SHPE.org

Yiddish Language

Forward, The

ORGANIZATIONS OFFERING RECRUITING TOOLS

A

B

C

D

E

F

H

I

J

L

M

N

Selected Titles from the Society for Human Resource Management (SHRM®)

Human Resource Essentials: Your Guide to Starting and Running the HR Function
By Lin Grensing-Pophal, SPHR

Legal, Effective References: How to Give and Get Them
By Wendy Bliss, JD, SPHR

Solutions for Human Resource Managers
By the SHRM Information Center Staff
in printed and e-book formats

Supervisor's Guide to Labor Relations
By T.O. Collier, Jr.

TO ORDER SHRM BOOKS

SHRM offers a member discount on all books that it publishes or sells. To order this or any other book published by the Society, contact the SHRMStore.™

ONLINE: www.shrm.org/shrmstore

BY PHONE: 800-444-5006 (option #1); or 770-442-8633 (ext. 362); or TDD 703-548-6999

BY FAX: 770-442-9742

BY MAIL: SHRM Distribution Center
P.O. Box 930132
Atlanta, GA 31193-0132
USA

DATE DUE

GAYLORD   PRINTED IN U.S.A.